HOW THE CLOUD REALLY WORKS

INSIDE THE PHYSICAL INFRASTRUCTURE OF THE DIGITAL WORLD

CLOUD MADE CLEAR
BOOK ONE

EUSTACE ASANGHANWA

VISIONARY QUILL

For my Wonderful Family

THE CLOUD IS A PLACE

INTRODUCTION

Somewhere in central Oregon, in a stretch of high desert where the nearest town is a twenty-minute drive and the nearest city is an hour beyond that, a building the size of a football field hums in the darkness.

It has no windows. No sign out front. No indication, from the road, of what happens inside. You could drive past it a thousand times and never give it a second thought. It looks like a warehouse, the kind of place that might store lumber or farm equipment. But behind its concrete walls, in long rows of metal racks that stretch from one end of the building to the other, tens of thousands of machines are working. They are answering questions, delivering videos, storing photographs, routing messages, processing payments, and keeping watch over bank accounts. All at the same time, all at extraordinary speed, all without rest.

It is two o'clock in the morning, and this building is wide awake.

A technician walks the floor between the racks, checking indicator lights. The air is cool, aggressively cool, held at a precise temperature by a cooling system that never shuts off. The sound is a steady, low roar, like standing inside the engine room of a ship. Somewhere overhead, thick bundles of fiber-optic cable run along cable trays, carrying pulses of light that represent the digital lives of millions of people. Your email. Your photos. Your last search. Your next message.

Right now, in this building, in the middle of the Oregon desert, a piece of your life is humming along, and you have no idea it's here.

This is the cloud.

Not a metaphor. Not an abstraction. Not a white, fluffy thing floating in the sky. The cloud is a place, thousands of places, in fact, scattered across the world in locations most people will never see. It is made of steel and silicon, glass and copper, concrete and electricity. It is maintained by human beings who work through the night, who swap out failing hard drives, who monitor dashboards of blinking lights, who respond to alarms at three in the morning so that when you wake up and reach for your phone, everything just works.

You already live in the cloud. You have for years. Every time you send a message, watch a video, check the weather, scroll through a feed, ask for directions, or tap "pay" at a checkout counter, you are reaching out across a vast, physical network to a machine in a building like the one in Oregon, and that machine is reaching back. The whole exchange takes less than a second. It feels instant. It feels effortless. It feels, if you think about it at all, like magic.

But it isn't magic. It's infrastructure.

That word, *infrastructure*, is the key to this book.

We don't usually think of the internet as infrastructure. We think of roads as infrastructure. Bridges. Power lines. Water pipes. These are the systems that run beneath daily life, mostly invisible, mostly taken for granted, noticed only when they fail. We flip a switch and the lights come on. We turn a tap and the water flows. We don't think about the power plant, the reservoir, the miles of cable and pipe that connect them to our homes. We just use them.

The cloud works the same way. It is a utility: a vast, global utility that delivers computing power, storage, and connectivity to anyone with a device and an internet connection. Just as you don't own a power plant but you plug into the electrical grid, you don't own a data center but you plug into the cloud. Someone else built the infrastructure. Someone else maintains it. Someone else keeps it running around the clock. You just use it.

The difference is that most people have at least a vague picture of how electricity works. They can imagine a power plant, a transmission line, a meter on the side of a house. But ask someone to picture "the cloud" and you'll usually get a shrug, a vague gesture upward, or a half-joke about it being "someone else's computer." Which isn't wrong, exactly, but it's like saying the electrical grid is "someone else's generator." Technically true. Practically useless. It tells you nothing about the staggering system that actually makes it all work.

This book is here to give you that picture.

What you're about to read is a guided tour of the most important infrastructure most people have never seen. We're going to start with the simplest possible question, what is the cloud, actually, and build from there, chapter by chapter, until you can see the entire system: the cables that run under oceans, the buildings that hum in deserts, the machines that store your memories, the networks that carry your voice across continents, and the people who keep it all running.

None of it requires technical expertise. You don't need to know how to code, or configure a server, or understand a network diagram. You just need to be curious. If you've ever wondered where your photos actually *go* when they disappear into the cloud, or how a video can travel from the other side of the world to your screen in less than a second, or why the internet almost never seems to go down, this book will answer those questions, clearly and honestly, with no jargon and no condescension.

Think of it as pulling back the curtain on a machine you use every day but have never really seen.

Once you see the cloud clearly, two things happen.

The first is awe. The system is astonishing. Right now, as you read this, hundreds of millions of people are streaming video simultaneously, each one watching something different, and it all works. Billions of messages are crossing the world every hour, arriving in the right hands, in the right order, usually in under a second. Your photos are being stored across multiple data centers on multiple continents, guarded by layers of encryption, backed up against every imaginable failure, and available to you on any device you pick up. The engineering behind this is breathtaking, and almost entirely invisible.

The second thing is understanding. Once the cloud stops being a vague metaphor and becomes a concrete, physical system in your mind, the digital world starts to make sense in a way it didn't before. You start to understand why some services are free and others cost money. You start to understand why the internet is fast in some places and slow in others. You start to understand the headlines about data centers and energy consumption, about undersea cables and geopolitics, about outages and reliability. You stop feeling like technology is something that happens *to* you, and start feeling like it's something you can *understand*.

That shift, from confusion to clarity, from passivity to understanding, is what this book is for.

A few words about what this book is *not*.

This is not a technical manual. There is no coding in these pages. There are no configuration guides, no diagrams of network protocols, no instructions for setting up a server. If you're an engineer, you'll find the explanations here deliberately simplified, because the goal is not precision for specialists. The goal is clarity for everyone.

This is also not a book about any specific company. You won't find comparisons of cloud providers or recommendations about which services to use. The cloud is bigger than any single company, and the principles that govern it are universal.

And this is not a book designed to frighten you. The internet has real challenges, security risks, privacy concerns, environmental costs, and we'll address all of them honestly. But the purpose is to help you *understand*, not to make you anxious. By the end, you should feel more informed and more in control, not less.

What this book *is*, above all, is a story. It's the story of the machine that runs beneath your fingertips: where it came from, how it works, what it's made of, and why it matters. It's a story about cables and buildings and electricity, about scale and redundancy and economics, about the people who built this thing and the people who keep it running. And it's a story about you, because this machine exists to serve you, and you deserve to understand it.

Here's how the tour works.

We'll start with the basics. Chapter 1 clears the fog around the word "cloud" and gives you the simplest, clearest mental model, one you'll carry through the rest of the book and, frankly, through the rest of your life. If you've ever struggled to explain what the cloud is, that chapter will fix it in a few pages.

Then we'll follow the journey. Chapter 2 traces what actually happens when you tap something on your phone: the entire trip, from your fingertip to a server on the other side of the world and back, in less than a second. It's the book's most important narrative, because it gives you the mental model that everything else builds on: the round trip between your device and the cloud.

From there, we go physical. Chapter 3 takes you beneath the ocean, where hundreds of thousands of miles of fiber-optic cable carry nearly all of the world's international internet traffic, a fact that astonishes almost everyone who hears it for the first time. Chapter 4 takes you inside a data center, with enough sensory detail that you'll be able to picture one with your eyes closed. Chapter 5 confronts the energy question honestly: what does it cost, in electricity and heat and water, to keep this machine running around the clock?

Then we explore how the system holds together. Chapter 6 explains the invisible engineering that keeps the internet running, why it almost never goes down, and what happens on the rare occasions it does. Chapter 7 answers the most personal question in the book: where is *my stuff*? Your photos, your documents, your memories — where are they, right now, and how are they being kept safe?

The final stretch zooms out. Chapter 8 explains the concept of scale: how the cloud can serve billions of people simultaneously, expanding and contracting like a living thing. Chapter 9 makes sense of the economics: why the cloud became the dominant model, why so many services are free, and what that means for you. And Chapter 10 puts people back at the center, following the technicians, cable crews, and engineers whose labor keeps the digital world alive.

By the time you reach the conclusion, you'll be able to do something most people can't: picture the internet. Not as a cloud. Not as a mystery. But as a machine that is vast, physical, human, and real.

One more thing before we begin.

I want you to try something. Take out your phone. Open any app. It doesn't matter which one. Tap something. A message, a photo, a search, a video. Watch the result appear on your screen.

Now consider what just happened.

In the fraction of a second between your tap and the response, a signal left your device, traveled through the air to a nearby antenna or router, entered a network of fiber-optic cables, crossed potentially thousands of miles, arrived at a building full of machines, was processed by a server, and the response was assembled, encrypted, and sent back along the same network, all the way to the screen in your hand.

Every piece of that journey is physical. Every piece has a location. Every piece was built by someone, is maintained by someone, and is powered by electricity generated somewhere.

You just reached out and touched a machine on the other side of the world. It answered you before you could blink. And you didn't even notice.

By the end of this book, you will.

Let's begin.

CHAPTER 1

THE CLOUD IS NOT MAGIC: WHAT IT ACTUALLY IS

Let's start with what most people think the cloud is.

If you ask around, and I have, many times, you'll get a fascinating range of answers. Some people gesture vaguely upward, as if the cloud is somewhere in the atmosphere. Some say it's "the internet," which isn't wrong but isn't particularly helpful either. Some will tell you it's where their photos go when their phone runs out of storage. A surprising number will admit, with varying degrees of sheepishness, that they have no idea what it means at all. They just know they use it.

The most common answer, and the one that comes closest, is this: "It's someone else's computer."

That's a fine starting point. It captures something real. But it's a bit like saying the electrical grid is "someone else's generator." Technically accurate, but it tells you almost nothing about the system: the power plants, the transmission lines, the transformers, the meters, the grid operators, the engineering of reliability that keeps the lights on twenty-four hours a day. Saying the cloud is "someone else's computer" is a sentence that ends a conversation. What follows is about starting one.

Here is the simplest definition of the cloud I can give you, and the one I'd like you to carry from here on:

> *The cloud is computing that happens somewhere else.*

That's it. When you use the cloud, you're using a computer, but not the one in your hand or on your desk. You're using a computer in a building you've never visited, owned by a company you may never have heard of, located in a place you'd probably never think to look. Your device sends a request over the internet. That distant computer does the work. And the result comes back to your screen.

Everything else, the data centers, the fiber-optic cables, the redundancy, the scale, the economics, is the story of how that simple idea became the foundation of modern digital life. But the core concept is this: work that used to happen on your device now happens on someone else's machine, far away, and the internet is the road between them.

. . .

Once you understand that, the cloud stops being a mystery. It becomes a system: one you can picture, understand, and think about clearly.

To appreciate why the cloud matters, and why it feels like the natural order of things rather than the radical shift it actually was, it helps to understand the history of how humans have related to computers. That history is shorter than you might think, and the cloud is only its most recent chapter.

THE MAINFRAME ERA

In the 1950s and 1960s, a computer was not something you owned. It was something you visited.

The machines of that era were enormous, filling entire rooms, consuming as much electricity as a small factory, and costing millions of dollars. They had names like UNIVAC and IBM System/360, and they were operated by teams of specialists in climate-controlled rooms with raised floors and restricted access. Only governments, major universities, and the largest corporations could afford them. If you worked at a company that had one, you didn't walk up to it and start typing. You prepared your work on punched cards, stiff rectangles of paper with holes punched in specific patterns, handed the stack to a technician, and waited. Hours later, sometimes a full day later, you got your results back, printed on long sheets of continuous paper.

. . .

The computer was a shared resource. Dozens or hundreds of people within an organization might depend on the same machine, submitting their jobs in batches, waiting their turns. The computing department controlled access, set priorities, and managed the machine. If you wanted to run a calculation, you didn't do it yourself; you asked the priesthood. That's what the computing staff were sometimes called, only half-jokingly: the priesthood of the mainframe.

If this sounds vaguely familiar, it should. The mainframe era established a pattern that would echo through the decades: powerful machines, in specialized buildings, doing work for many people at once, managed by professionals who kept the machinery running. That pattern went away for a while. Then it came back, transformed, democratized, and scaled beyond anything the mainframe builders could have imagined. It came back as the cloud.

THE PERSONAL COMPUTER REVOLUTION

In the late 1970s and 1980s, something extraordinary happened: the computer shrank.

The microprocessor, a single chip capable of doing the work that had once required a room-sized machine, made it possible to put real computing power into a box that fit on a desk. Companies with names like Apple, IBM, and Commodore began selling machines to ordinary people for a few thousand dollars. The personal computer arrived, and it changed everything.

Suddenly, you didn't need access to a mainframe. You didn't need to submit punched cards or wait for the computing department. You had your own machine, sitting on your desk, responding to your commands in real time. You could write documents. You could build spreadsheets. You could play games, design graphics, manage your finances, and print letters, all without asking anyone for permission.

The PC era produced an explosion of creativity and productivity. Word processors replaced typewriters. Spreadsheets replaced paper ledgers. Databases replaced filing cabinets. Millions of people who had never touched a mainframe became computer users. The computer moved from the locked room to the living room, and computing ceased to be the domain of specialists. It became personal.

But the personal computer model had a cost that wasn't immediately obvious: everything was on you. *You* maintained the machine. *You* installed the software and figured out the error messages. *You* backed up the files, or, more commonly, you didn't, and lost everything when the hard drive failed. If the machine broke, your data went with it. There was no safety net. There was no priesthood. There was no climate-controlled room with backup systems and trained operators. There was just you and your box, for better and for worse.

. . .

Freedom had a price, and the price was fragility.

THE NETWORKED ERA

In the 1990s, the internet changed the picture again.

Personal computers gained the ability to connect, to each other and to distant servers. Email, which had existed in primitive form on mainframes and university networks for years, suddenly became something ordinary people used. You had an email address. You could send a message to anyone in the world who had one. The information didn't live on your computer; it lived on a mail server, run by your internet provider or your employer, accessible from any machine you logged into.

The World Wide Web appeared, and with it, websites: pages of information stored on servers, accessible to anyone with a browser and a connection. Shopping moved online. Banking moved online. News moved online. The server, a distant computer you connected to through the internet, became a fixture of daily life, even if most people didn't think of it in those terms.

This was the awkward middle period, not quite local, not quite cloud. Your computer still did most of the work. Your files still lived on your hard drive. Your software still came on discs that you installed yourself. But increasingly, the most valuable things you did with your computer involved reaching out to someone else's machine: checking email, browsing the web, searching for information, shopping, communicating. The center of gravity was shifting, slowly, unevenly, from the device in front of you to the network it was connected to.

People began to get comfortable with the idea that some of their data lived *somewhere else*, even if they couldn't have told you exactly where. The groundwork was being laid, though nobody called it the cloud yet.

AND THEN CAME THE CLOUD

In the early 2000s, a handful of companies, the ones running the largest computing operations in the world to power their own products, realized something surprising. To serve hundreds of millions of users, they had built computing infrastructure on a scale that no one had attempted before: vast data centers filled with tens of thousands of servers, connected by high-speed networks, managed by sophisticated software that could allocate resources dynamically. And they had built more capacity than they needed at any given moment, because they had to plan for peak demand, the busiest hour of the busiest day.

The insight was simple: why not rent out the excess? If your data centers have capacity sitting idle, and other companies need computing power, why not let them use yours, for a fee, on demand, with no long-term commitment?

. . .

The idea wasn't entirely new. Mainframes had offered shared computing decades earlier. Time-sharing services in the 1960s and 1970s had let multiple users share a single machine. But the scale was different now. The accessibility was different. The pricing was different. For the first time, any company, or any person, could rent computing power by the hour, storage by the gigabyte, and services by the request, without buying a single machine, without visiting a data center, without even knowing where the servers were located. The barrier to entry collapsed. A college student with a credit card could access the same computing infrastructure as a multinational corporation, paying only for what they used.

The cloud didn't replace the personal computer. You still have a device in your hand. But the device is increasingly a window, a screen that displays the work being done somewhere else. Your photos are stored in the cloud. Your email runs in the cloud. Your documents, your messages, your music, your maps. All of it lives on distant machines, maintained by someone else, accessible from any device you pick up.

The pendulum swung. Computing started in centralized machines (mainframes), moved to personal machines (PCs), passed through a networked phase (the internet era), and arrived at a new form of centralized computing, but this time, accessible to everyone, from everywhere, at a cost that approaches zero.

The cloud is not a break from history. It's a return to an old idea, shared, centralized computing, made radically better by everything that came between.

What did this shift feel like for ordinary people? Mostly, it felt like things getting easier.

Remember the personal computer era, the years when everything was on you? Think about what it was like to manage your own technology in, say, 2003. Your photos lived on your computer's hard drive. If you wanted to share them, you burned them onto a CD or emailed them one at a time. Your music was a collection of files that you'd spent hours ripping from CDs or downloading from the internet, organized in folders that you maintained yourself. If your hard drive died, the music was gone. Your documents were saved locally. If you wanted to work on a file from two different computers, you copied it onto a USB drive and carried it between them, hoping you remembered which version was the latest.

Now think about today. Your photos are backed up automatically. Your music is a streaming subscription: every song ever recorded, available instantly, on any device. Your documents live in the cloud and sync across your laptop, your phone, and your tablet. You don't carry USB drives. You don't burn CDs. You don't worry about which version of a file is the latest, because there's only one version, and it lives on a server that every device checks against.

. . .

The transition from the old world to this one didn't happen overnight. It crept in, app by app, service by service, year by year. Most people didn't notice the moment when their digital lives moved from local devices to the cloud. There was no announcement. No switch was flipped. The cloud just gradually became the place where everything lived, and the experience became so smooth that the underlying infrastructure disappeared from view.

That invisibility is, in many ways, the cloud's greatest achievement. The best infrastructure is the kind you don't have to think about. You don't think about the water treatment plant when you turn on the tap. You don't think about the power grid when you flip a light switch. And you don't think about the data center when you open your email. It just works.

But looking at what you usually don't think about is exactly the point, and now you know the history that brought us here. From mainframes to personal computers to the networked internet to the cloud, each era solved the problems of the one before it and created new ones. The cloud solved the fragility and isolation of personal computing. What new challenges it creates, in power, in concentration, in privacy, are questions the rest of these pages, and the rest of this series, will explore.

The best analogy I've found for the cloud is one that most people already live with: the difference between cooking at home and ordering from a restaurant.

. . .

When you cook at home, you need a kitchen, equipment, ingredients, and the skill to put it all together. Everything happens under your roof. If your stove breaks, dinner isn't happening. If you don't have the right ingredients, you're out of luck. You are entirely self-reliant, which is great when it works and a real problem when it doesn't.

When you order from a restaurant, you get the same result, food on your table, but the kitchen, the equipment, the ingredients, the chef, and the expertise are all somewhere else. You don't need to own any of it. You don't need to maintain any of it. You just place an order, and the meal arrives.

Cloud computing is ordering from the restaurant. Your device places the order. A powerful computer somewhere else prepares the result. And it arrives on your screen, usually in less than a second.

The kitchen is real. The chef is real. The ingredients are real. You just don't see any of it.

If that's all the cloud is, computing that happens somewhere else, why did it take over the world?

The answer has less to do with technology than you might think. It has to do with a simple economic truth that changed everything: for most people and most purposes, it's far cheaper and far easier to use someone else's computer than to own and maintain your own.

Think about it from a company's perspective. Before the cloud, if you wanted to run a website or an app, you had to buy your own servers. Physical machines, sitting in a room, that you owned and maintained. You had to guess how many you'd need, and guessing was agonizing. Buy too few, and your service would crash when too many people showed up. Buy too many, and you'd waste money on machines that sat idle most of the time. You needed staff to maintain them, space to house them, electricity to power them, and cooling systems to keep them from overheating. Running your own computing infrastructure was expensive, complicated, and risky.

And the timing was brutal. Buying servers meant committing capital months in advance: ordering equipment, waiting for delivery, installing and configuring hardware, all before you could serve a single user. If your business grew faster than expected, you couldn't get more capacity quickly enough. If it grew slower, you were stuck with equipment you'd already paid for. The mismatch between the speed of business and the speed of hardware procurement was one of the great frustrations of the pre-cloud era.

The cloud changed that equation entirely. Instead of buying servers, you rent computing power, as much as you need, for as long as you need it. Need more capacity because your app went viral? The cloud scales up in minutes. Traffic died down? It scales back, and you stop paying for what you're not using. You don't buy equipment. You don't hire server technicians. You don't worry about hardware failures. Someone else handles all of that.

This is the fundamental shift: **from owning to renting**.

And it's not a new idea in the broader sweep of history either. The shift from owning to renting has happened before, with electricity, and the parallel is so close that it's almost eerie.

In the late nineteenth century, if your factory needed electricity, you built your own power plant. Literally. You installed a steam engine or a water wheel, connected it to a generator, ran wires through your building, and produced your own power. Every factory was its own electrical utility. The machinery was expensive. The fuel was expensive. The engineers who maintained it were expensive. And the system was wildly inefficient; each factory generated power in isolation, with no way to share excess capacity or draw extra power during surges.

Then came the electrical grid. Central power stations, built by utilities, generated electricity at enormous scale and distributed it through networks of transmission lines to factories, businesses, and homes. Suddenly, a factory didn't need its own generator. It plugged into the grid, flipped a switch, and paid for what it used. The capital expense of building and maintaining a private power plant was replaced by a monthly utility bill. The savings were so dramatic that within a few decades, private power generation all but disappeared. Why own the machinery when you could rent the output?

The parallel is almost exact. Before the grid, electricity was something you made yourself, at enormous cost. After the grid, it was something you plugged into, paying only for what you used. Before the cloud, computing was something you owned, at enormous cost: servers, buildings, staff, electricity, cooling. After the cloud, it was something you plugged into, paying only for what you used, scaling up or down as needed, with someone else handling the machinery.

The cloud did the same thing for computing that the electrical grid did for power. It turned a capital expense into a utility bill. And just like electrification, which transformed manufacturing, transportation, entertainment, and daily life in ways that nobody fully predicted, cloud computing has transformed the digital world in ways that are still unfolding.

This is where the central metaphor comes in, and it's one worth holding onto, because it will keep coming back throughout the series.

> *The cloud is a utility: like electricity, like water, like the phone network.*

. . .

You don't own a power plant. You plug into the grid. You don't own a water treatment facility. You turn on the tap. You don't own a telephone exchange. You make a call. In each case, someone else built and maintains the infrastructure. You pay for what you use. And it works so reliably that you almost never think about it.

The cloud works the same way. Someone else built the data centers. Someone else laid the fiber-optic cables. Someone else maintains the servers, manages the cooling systems, monitors for failures, and responds to problems in the middle of the night. You just open an app, and it works.

This metaphor isn't perfect; no metaphor is. The electrical grid is regulated as a public utility, and the cloud mostly isn't. The grid has been around for over a century, and the cloud is still relatively young. But the core insight holds: the cloud is shared infrastructure that you access on demand, without owning any of it.

And just like the electrical grid, the cloud has become so woven into daily life that most people don't notice it's there, until it stops working.

There's one more thing worth making clear before we move on, because it trips people up more than almost anything else about the cloud.

The cloud is not *one* thing. It's not a single computer, a single company, or a single location. It's a way of doing things, a model for how computing works. When someone says "it's in the cloud," they mean the data or the processing lives on a remote server somewhere, accessible over the internet. But that server could be in Oregon, or Virginia, or Ireland, or Singapore. It could be owned by one of the handful of very large companies that operate the world's biggest cloud infrastructure, or it could be run by a smaller provider you've never heard of.

The cloud is a system, not a place, except that the system is made of real places. That's the beautiful paradox of it, and it's the tension that drives everything that follows. The cloud feels abstract, ethereal, somewhere "up there." But every piece of it is physical. Every file you store in the cloud is sitting on a hard drive in a building. Every search you run is processed by a real machine. Every video you stream is delivered by real servers through real cables.

The cloud is not magic. It's infrastructure — vast, physical, ingeniously designed, and maintained by people. And it's the latest chapter in a story that started with room-sized mainframes and punched cards, passed through the PC revolution and the birth of the internet, and arrived at the single most powerful computing system humanity has ever built — one that happens to be invisible to most of the people who use it.

. . .

Now you know what it is. The next step is to see it in action: to follow a single tap on your phone, from the moment your finger touches the screen to the moment the answer appears. The whole trip takes less than a second. But in that second, something extraordinary happens — and once you see it, you'll never look at your phone the same way again.

CHAPTER 2

THE JOURNEY OF A SINGLE TAP

You're standing in a coffee shop. Your phone is in your hand. You open a messaging app and tap on a photo your friend sent you, a picture from their vacation, somewhere sunny. The image fills your screen. You smile. You type a quick reply. The whole thing takes maybe three seconds.

It felt like nothing happened. But in those three seconds, something extraordinary took place, a journey so fast and so intricate that describing it in real time would be like trying to narrate a bolt of lightning.

That photo wasn't on your phone. It was sitting on a server, a computer in a data center, possibly thousands of miles from the coffee shop where you're standing. When you tapped the screen, your phone sent a request across a series of networks, through cables and switches and routers, to that distant machine. The server found the photo, packaged it up, encrypted it, and sent it back along a different route, racing through fiber-optic cables at nearly the speed of light, until it arrived at the antenna nearest to you, leaped through the air as a radio signal, and landed on the screen in your hand.

The whole round trip, from your fingertip to a machine on the other side of the country and back, took less than a second. Probably less than half a second. You didn't notice. You weren't supposed to.

But now you're going to see it.

Every time you use the internet, every message, every search, every video, every purchase, you are sending a request to a distant machine and receiving a response. That loop is the heartbeat of the cloud. Once you can picture it, the entire digital world starts to make sense.

Let's follow the tap.

It begins with your finger on glass.

When you tap your phone's screen, you're pressing against a thin layer of capacitive glass that detects the electrical charge in your skin. The phone registers the exact location of the touch and matches it to whatever was displayed at that point on the screen, in this case, your friend's photo thumbnail. The app now knows what you want: *show me this image, full size.*

But the app doesn't have the image. Not the full version, anyway. Your phone might have stored a tiny, compressed preview, just enough to show the thumbnail in your conversation, but the actual high-resolution photo is sitting on a server far away. To get it, your phone needs to ask for it.

So the app composes a request. Think of it as a very short, very specific letter. It contains a few essential pieces of information: who you are (your account, verified by a token that proves you're logged in), what you want (this specific image, identified by a unique code), and where to send the response (back to your device, identified by its network address). The request is tiny, just a few hundred bytes, a whisper of data, but it contains everything the server needs to understand what you're asking for.

Now that request needs to leave your phone and find its way to the server that has the photo. The first step is getting off the device entirely.

If you're connected to the coffee shop's Wi-Fi, your phone transmits the request as a radio signal to a small box mounted somewhere on the wall or ceiling, the wireless router. That router is the first link in the chain. It receives the signal, converts it from radio waves into electrical pulses, and passes it along through a cable, usually an ethernet cable running through the walls, to a device that connects the coffee shop to the wider internet.

If you're not on Wi-Fi, your phone sends the request as a different kind of radio signal, a cellular signal, to the nearest cell tower. That tower might be on a rooftop a few blocks away or on a pole beside a highway. Either way, it receives your signal and feeds it into the same broader network.

The point is the same: your request has left your phone and entered the physical network of cables, switches, and routers that make up the internet. It's no longer a signal in the air. It's a pulse of light or electricity traveling through a wire. And it has a long way to go.

Here's where things get interesting. Your request knows where it wants to go; it has the address of the server that holds the photo. But it doesn't know the *route*. The internet doesn't work like a direct phone line between your device and the server. It works more like the postal system.

When you mail a letter, you don't drive it to the recipient's house yourself. You drop it in a mailbox, and the postal service takes over. Your letter goes to a local sorting facility, where it's read, sorted, and sent to another facility, maybe across town, maybe across the country. At each stop, someone looks at the address and decides where to send it next. Eventually, after several hops, the letter arrives at the recipient's door.

The internet works the same way, except the sorting facilities are called *routers*, and they process your request in millionths of a second instead of hours.

Your request leaves the coffee shop's network and hits the first router, a device operated by your internet service provider. That router looks at the destination address and makes a decision: I don't have a direct connection to that server, but I know which direction to send this. It forwards the request to the next router, which makes the same decision, and so on. Each step is called a "hop," and a typical request might make ten or twenty hops before reaching its destination.

This process happens so fast that it feels instantaneous. But each hop is a real, physical event: your data arriving at a real machine, being read, being forwarded, arriving at the next machine. If you could slow time down enough to watch, you'd see your request bouncing from building to building, city to city, sometimes country to country, like a pinball finding its way through a machine.

There's a piece of history behind this, because it explains *why* the internet works this way, and why the design turned out to be so resilient.

. . .

In the 1960s, engineers working on early computer networks faced a problem: how do you send data between two computers that aren't directly connected? The telephone system of the time used *circuit switching*: when you made a phone call, a dedicated line was opened between you and the person you were calling, and that line stayed open for the entire conversation. It was reliable, but wasteful. The line was reserved for you even during the silences, and if the line was cut, the call dropped.

A researcher named Paul Baran at the RAND Corporation proposed a radically different approach: instead of opening a dedicated line, break the data into small pieces, *packets*, and send each one independently through the network. Each packet would carry the address of its destination, and each router along the way would forward it toward that destination using whatever route was available at that moment. The packets might take different paths. They might arrive out of order. But the receiving computer would reassemble them into the original message, and the result would be the same, except that no single route needed to stay open, and no single break in the network could stop the message from getting through.

This idea, packet switching, became the foundation of the internet. It's why your request doesn't need a dedicated line to the server. It's broken into packets, each one independently routed, each one finding its own way through the network. If one route is congested, the packets flow through another. If a cable is cut, the packets reroute automatically. The system was designed, from its earliest conception, to be unkillable, to keep working even when parts of the network failed. That design decision, made over sixty years ago, is the reason your photo arrived in under a second even though the path between your phone and the server crosses dozens of independent networks.

But before any of that routing can happen, your phone needs to solve a problem that most people have never thought about: it needs to figure out where the server actually *is*.

When you tapped that photo, your app knew it needed to contact a server, let's call it "photos.messagingservice.com." That's a name, not an address. It's like knowing you want to mail a letter to "the Johnson house" without knowing the street address. You need a way to look it up.

This is where the Domain Name System, DNS, comes in. DNS is the internet's phone book. It translates human-readable names (like "photos.messagingservice.com") into machine-readable addresses (like 172.217.14.99, a string of numbers called an IP address that identifies a specific server on the network).

In the early days of the internet, this translation wasn't needed, because there were so few computers that a simple text file, maintained by hand, listed all of them. As the network grew from dozens of machines to thousands to millions to billions, that approach became impossible. DNS was created in the 1980s as a distributed, automated system that could handle the lookup at any scale. Today, DNS servers around the world process trillions of lookups every day, and the system is so reliable that most people have never heard of it.

Here's how it works for your request. Your phone sends a quick side query to a DNS server, a specialized computer whose only job is to answer the question "what's the address for this name?" The DNS server checks its records, finds the matching IP address, and sends it back. Your phone now knows exactly where to send the request: not to a vague "server somewhere" but to a specific machine at a specific address on the network.

This lookup happens before anything else. It's so fast, usually a few milliseconds, that you never notice it. But without it, your request would have nowhere to go. DNS is one of those invisible systems that the entire internet depends on, running silently in the background, billions of times a day, converting the names humans remember into the numbers machines need. Think of it as the receptionist who answers the phone before connecting your call. You never see them, but without them, nothing gets through.

Your request has now left your phone, passed through the coffee shop's router, traveled across several hops through the network, and arrived, at last, at a data center.

You already know what a data center is: a building full of servers, often in a remote location, humming around the clock. Your request has crossed the threshold, digitally speaking, passing through the facility's perimeter firewalls and security layers, arriving at the edge of its internal network. In the physical world, this building might be a thousand miles from the coffee shop where you're standing. In the digital world, the distance was covered in milliseconds. Your request is now inside the building, traveling at the speed of light through internal fiber-optic cables, heading toward the machines that will answer it.

But it doesn't go straight to a single server. First, it encounters something called a load balancer.

Think of a load balancer as a maître d' at a very busy restaurant. You walk in and say, "I'd like a table." The maître d' doesn't seat you at a random table or at the first one they see. They check which sections are busy, which waiters have capacity, and which tables are available, and then they seat you in the spot that keeps the whole restaurant running smoothly.

A load balancer does the same thing with incoming requests. The messaging service doesn't run on one server; it runs on hundreds or thousands of servers, all doing the same job. When your request arrives, the load balancer checks which server has the lightest workload and routes your request there. This way, no single machine gets overwhelmed, even when millions of people are using the service at the same time.

This is such a simple idea, spread the work around, but it's one of the things that makes the cloud possible at scale. Without load balancing, any popular service would collapse under its own success. With it, millions of requests are handled simultaneously, each one routed to the machine best positioned to respond.

Your request has been routed to a specific server. Now that server goes to work.

First, it checks your identity. That token your app included in the request, the one that proves you're logged in, gets verified against the service's authentication system. Is this a real user? Is their session still active? Do they have permission to see this photo? These checks happen in microseconds, but they're essential. Without them, anyone could request anyone else's photos.

Once your identity is confirmed, the server processes the actual request: find this photo and send it back.

The photo itself might not be stored on this particular server. In large systems, data is spread across many machines, sometimes across multiple data centers in different cities or even different countries. The server that received your request might need to call another server to retrieve the actual image file. That internal request happens over the data center's private network, an extremely fast, high-bandwidth connection between machines that sit in the same building or cluster of buildings.

. . .

The photo is found. But before it's sent back to you, a few more things happen. The server checks what kind of device you're using and what kind of connection you're on. If you're on a fast Wi-Fi network with a large screen, it might send the full-resolution image. If you're on a slower cellular connection or a smaller screen, it might send a compressed version, still sharp enough to look good, but smaller in size so it arrives faster. This optimization happens automatically, behind the scenes, tailored to your specific situation.

Finally, the response is assembled: the image data, packaged with a few instructions telling your app how to display it, encrypted so that nobody can intercept it along the way.

The server sends it back.

The return journey is, in some ways, the mirror image of the outbound trip. The response leaves the data center, enters the network, and hops from router to router, but not necessarily the same routers it passed through on the way in. The internet is dynamic; routes shift constantly based on traffic, congestion, and availability. The return path might be completely different from the outbound path, and neither your phone nor the server knows or cares. All that matters is that the response arrives.

. . .

And it does. The data reaches the cell tower or Wi-Fi router nearest to you, is transmitted as a radio signal through the air, and arrives at your phone. Your messaging app receives the response, decrypts it, processes the image data, and renders the photo on your screen.

You see your friend's vacation photo in full detail. The whole thing, from tap to image, took less than a second.

Let's slow down and appreciate what just happened.

In under a second, your phone composed a request, translated a server name into a numerical address using a global lookup system, sent the request through the air to a local antenna, passed it through a chain of routers across potentially thousands of miles of cable, each one independently making a routing decision in microseconds, delivered it to a specific building, where a load balancer directed it to one of thousands of available machines, which verified your identity against an authentication database, located the image across a distributed storage system spanning multiple facilities, optimized the image for your specific device and connection speed, encrypted the response, and sent it back along a different chain of routers and cables, through the air, to the screen in your hand.

Dozens of machines were involved. Thousands of miles of cable. Multiple layers of software. Multiple security checks.

The request was broken into packets, each one independently routed, each one potentially taking a different path through the network. And the whole thing was invisible to you.

Consider, for a moment, how improbable this would have seemed to someone in 1990. The idea that a device in your pocket could silently communicate with a machine on the other side of the continent, retrieve a high-resolution photograph, and display it on a handheld screen, all in less time than it takes to draw a breath, would have sounded like science fiction. The individual technologies existed in primitive form: networks, servers, digital photography, mobile devices. But the idea that they would converge into a seamless, instantaneous, globally accessible system that billions of people would use without thinking? That was beyond anyone's realistic expectation.

And yet here you are, doing it dozens of times a day, barely noticing.

This is the round trip. It happens every time you use the internet. Every search, every message, every video, every map request, every payment, every notification: all of them follow this same fundamental pattern. Your device sends a request to a distant machine, and the machine sends back a response. The details change, the servers are different, the data is different, the processing is different, but the structure is the same.

. . .

Once you see this loop, you start to see it everywhere. When you search for something, your query travels to a server that runs it against an index of billions of pages and sends back the results. When you stream a video, your device sends a continuous series of requests and receives a continuous stream of responses, each one carrying a fraction of a second of footage. When your phone buzzes with a notification, a server somewhere has pushed a message to your device through a standing connection that's always open, waiting.

Every interaction you have with the digital world is a conversation: your device asking, a distant machine answering, across a physical network of cables, routers, and servers, at a speed that makes the whole thing feel like it's happening inside your phone.

It's not. It's happening everywhere.

There's one more thing to notice about this journey, because it reveals something fundamental about the way the internet is designed.

No single entity controls the entire trip.

Your phone connects to a local network, the coffee shop's Wi-Fi or your cellular provider. That network connects to a regional internet service provider. That provider connects to a larger backbone network. The backbone connects to the data center's network. Each segment is owned and operated by a different company, using different equipment, under different management. Your request passes through all of them seamlessly, because they all agree to speak the same language: a set of shared rules called protocols.

Protocols are the invisible agreements that make the internet work. They define how data is formatted, how it's addressed, how it's broken into small packets for transmission, and how it's reassembled at the other end. They ensure that a request from any device, on any network, can reach any server, anywhere in the world. Without protocols, the internet would be a collection of isolated networks that couldn't talk to each other. With them, it's one interconnected system — the largest machine humanity has ever built.

You don't need to know the names of these protocols or how they work internally. What matters is the principle: the internet is not controlled by any single company or government. It's a cooperative system, millions of independent networks that have agreed to connect to each other and follow shared rules. Your request passes through many hands on its journey, and each one carries it faithfully forward, because that's how the system works.

This decentralized design is one of the reasons the internet is so resilient. If one route fails, traffic reroutes automatically through another. If one network goes down, the rest keep working. There is no single switch that turns the whole internet off, no central hub that everything depends on.

This wasn't an accident. It was a design choice, and it traces back to the internet's earliest ancestor: ARPANET, a network funded by the U.S. Department of Defense in the late 1960s. ARPANET connected a handful of university and government computers using the packet-switching technology just discussed. It was small, four nodes at launch in 1969, but it proved that independent computers, on separate networks, could communicate reliably using shared rules.

Over the following decades, ARPANET's principles, packet switching, decentralized routing, shared protocols, were adopted by other networks, which gradually connected to each other. The "inter-networking" of these separate networks produced, eventually, the *internet*: a network of networks, with no central authority, no single owner, and no master switch. The architecture that carries your photo request today is a direct descendant of the architecture that carried the first messages between UCLA and Stanford in 1969. The scale has changed beyond recognition. The principles haven't.

The full picture of that resilience comes later. For now, notice that the simplicity of your experience, tap, wait, result, is made possible by an astonishing complexity underneath. Hundreds of systems, dozens of networks, thousands of miles of cable, all coordinating perfectly in under a second, every time.

Think about the last time you used your phone to look something up, a fact, a restaurant, a weather forecast, anything. You probably didn't think about it at all. You just tapped and got an answer.

But here's what actually happened: you held a small glass rectangle up to your face, and it sent an invisible signal through the air. That signal entered a network of cables that stretched across your city, across the country, possibly across an ocean. It arrived at a building you've never seen, where a machine you'll never touch found the answer and sent it back, through different cables, different routers, different networks, until it emerged from the air and landed on your screen.

The whole thing took less time than it takes to blink.

You did this casually, without thinking, probably while waiting for your coffee. But what you actually did was reach out across a continent and touch a machine, and it touched you back. You had a conversation with a computer on the other side of the world, using a network of cables and light and electricity that spans the entire planet.

That network has a history. It descends from a four-node experiment in 1969. It was built on the idea that data should be broken into packets and routed independently, an idea that seemed impractical when it was first proposed and now carries the weight of the global economy. It was designed to survive disruption, and it does, handling billions of conversations simultaneously, rerouting around failures, scaling to meet demand that the original designers never imagined.

That's not a small thing. That's one of the most remarkable achievements in human history. It just doesn't feel remarkable because it happens so fast, so reliably, and so often that it's become ordinary.

Making it un-ordinary again, seeing the extraordinary system that hides behind the ordinary experience, is exactly the point.

Now that you've seen the journey, the next step is to see the roads. Next, we go beneath the ocean, where hundreds of thousands of miles of fiber-optic cable carry the world's data through pulses of light, laid by specialized ships, repaired by divers, and occasionally chewed on by sharks.

The physical internet is even stranger than you think. Let's go see it.

CHAPTER 3

THE WIRES BENEATH THE WORLD: CABLES, FIBER, AND HOW DATA TRAVELS

Here is a fact that surprises almost everyone who hears it for the first time: nearly all of the world's international internet traffic travels through cables lying on the floor of the ocean.

Not satellites. Not radio waves. Not some invisible signal bouncing between towers. Cables. Physical, tangible cables, some no thicker than a garden hose, lying in the silt and sediment at the bottom of the Atlantic, the Pacific, the Indian Ocean, and the Mediterranean Sea. Hundreds of thousands of miles of them, connecting continents, carrying the conversations and commerce and culture of the entire planet through pulses of light moving at nearly the speed of light.

When you send a message to someone in another country, there is a very good chance that your words travel underwater. When you stream a movie made on the other side of the world, the data crosses an ocean floor. When you video-call a colleague in another time zone, your face, broken into light, encoded as data, races through a glass thread thinner than a human hair, along the bottom of the sea, through the dark and the cold and the crushing pressure, and emerges on the other side of the planet in a fraction of a second.

The internet feels wireless. It feels weightless. It feels like it exists in the air, or in space, or nowhere in particular. But the physical reality is the opposite. The internet is a machine made of glass and copper, steel and concrete, electricity and light, and its most critical arteries run through the most inhospitable environment on Earth.

What follows is the story of the roads that carry your data, from the ocean floor to your front door.

Let's start at the bottom of the ocean, and in the nineteenth century.

The idea of stretching a cable across the Atlantic was, by the standards of the 1850s, somewhere between audacious and insane. The ocean between Ireland and Newfoundland was two thousand miles wide, two and a half miles deep in places, and almost entirely unmapped beneath the surface. No one had ever laid a cable across anything close to that distance. The technology for insulating wire against seawater was primitive. The ships available were barely adequate for the task. And the man who decided to try it anyway, an American businessman named Cyrus Field, had no engineering background at all. He was a retired paper merchant with money, conviction, and a talent for persuading other people to share his vision.

Field spent more than a decade on the project. He crossed the Atlantic dozens of times to raise capital and coordinate logistics. He assembled a team of the best electrical engineers and maritime experts of the era. He convinced the British and American governments to lend warships for the cable-laying expeditions.

The first serious attempt, in 1857, failed when the cable snapped in deep water after a few hundred miles. A second attempt in 1858 succeeded, barely. Two ships, starting from the middle of the Atlantic and sailing in opposite directions, managed to lay a continuous cable from Ireland to Newfoundland. On August 16, 1858, Queen Victoria sent a congratulatory message to President James Buchanan over the new cable. It took sixteen hours to transmit, each letter painstakingly tapped out in Morse code, the signal faint and unreliable across two thousand miles of poorly insulated wire.

The public celebrated. Fireworks were launched. Church bells rang. The New York Times declared it "the most wonderful achievement of this victorious century." Cities held parades. The cable was hailed as a miracle of human ingenuity.

It lasted three weeks.

. . .

The insulation degraded. The operators, desperate to push signals across the weakening cable, cranked up the voltage, which accelerated the deterioration. By early September, the cable was dead. Two thousand miles of copper and gutta-percha insulation, lying useless on the ocean floor. Millions of dollars lost. Field's reputation in tatters.

But he didn't stop. He spent the next several years refining the technology: better insulation, better cable design, better laying techniques. The American Civil War interrupted his plans. A second cable-laying attempt in 1865, using the largest ship in the world, Isambard Kingdom Brunel's *Great Eastern*, failed when the cable snapped in mid-ocean. But in 1866, the *Great Eastern* tried again, and this time it worked. The cable held. And then the ship sailed back, grappled the broken 1865 cable from the ocean floor, spliced it, and completed a second working line.

By the end of 1866, two functioning telegraph cables connected Europe and North America. Messages that had once taken weeks to cross the Atlantic by ship now crossed in minutes. The world shrank overnight. Financial markets synchronized. Diplomacy accelerated. News became global. The undersea cable had done what the printing press did for information and the railroad did for trade: it collapsed distance.

The reason for telling this story at length is that the modern internet follows the same path, literally. The undersea fiber-optic cables that carry your data across the Atlantic today follow routes that were first mapped by Cyrus Field's surveyors in the 1850s. The landing stations in Ireland and Newfoundland that anchor modern cables are descendants of the stations where Field's telegraph cables came ashore. The industry that lays and maintains today's fiber-optic cables, the ships, the crews, the repair techniques, evolved directly from the industry that Field's project created.

The technology has changed beyond recognition. Glass fiber instead of copper wire. Laser light instead of electrical pulses. Terabits per second instead of a few words per minute. But the fundamental human achievement is the same: stretching a line of communication across the bottom of the ocean, connecting continents that would otherwise be separated by weeks of travel. Cyrus Field would recognize what we're doing. He just wouldn't believe how fast it's become.

The modern version of Field's cable is a miracle of engineering, and it carries data at a rate the Victorian engineers could not have imagined. A single modern undersea fiber-optic cable can transmit tens of terabits per second, enough to carry millions of simultaneous video calls, hundreds of millions of web pages, and billions of messages, all at once, all in real time.

The cable itself is deceptively simple in appearance. At its core are thin strands of glass fiber, usually between eight and sixteen pairs of them, each one capable of carrying enormous quantities of data as pulses of laser light. These fibers are bundled together and wrapped in layers of protection: a waterproof coating, steel wire for strength, copper tubing for power (the repeaters along the cable's length need electricity), and an outer sheath of polyethylene to protect against the ocean environment. The final product, in deep ocean, is roughly the diameter of a garden hose. In shallower coastal waters, where the cable is more vulnerable to anchors, fishing trawls, and human activity, additional armoring, layers of steel wire and tar, can make it as thick as a soda can.

That's it. The backbone of the global internet, the system that carries your messages across continents, is a tube the size of a garden hose, filled with hair-thin glass threads, lying on the ocean floor.

How do you lay a cable across the bottom of an ocean?

The process is one of the most extraordinary feats of engineering that almost nobody has heard of. It begins with a survey, sometimes taking years, to map the proposed route along the seafloor. The cable needs to avoid underwater mountains, active fault zones, areas of heavy fishing, and regions where the seabed is too rocky or too soft. The ideal path follows gentle, sandy slopes where the cable can rest undisturbed for decades.

Once the route is mapped, the cable is manufactured. This typically happens at specialized factories, only a handful exist in the world, where thousands of miles of cable are produced, tested, and coiled into enormous tanks aboard a cable-laying ship. These ships are purpose-built vessels, some of the most specialized in any maritime fleet. They carry the cable in circular tanks below deck, feeding it out over the stern as the ship moves slowly along the planned route, at a pace of a few miles per hour.

The laying process itself can take weeks or months, depending on the length of the route. The ship crawls across the ocean, paying out cable behind it in a continuous stream. In deep water, where the ocean can be three or four miles deep, the cable simply sinks to the bottom under its own weight, settling into the sediment. In shallower coastal areas, a plow attached to the ship buries the cable a meter or two beneath the seabed to protect it from anchors and trawl nets.

Along the way, at intervals of roughly forty to sixty miles, the cable includes repeaters: small amplifiers sealed in titanium-and-steel housings that boost the optical signal as it travels. Light weakens over distance, even in the purest glass, and without these repeaters the signal would fade to nothing long before it reached the other side. Each repeater is designed to operate for twenty-five years or more at the bottom of the ocean, without maintenance, without repair, without anyone ever touching it again. The engineering required to achieve that kind of reliability, in that kind of environment, is quietly staggering.

When the cable reaches the far shore, it's pulled up through a landing station, a nondescript building, usually near the coast, where it connects to the terrestrial network. From there, the data flows into the land-based fiber and cable systems that carry it to cities, neighborhoods, and eventually to your device.

The whole operation, from survey to landing, can cost hundreds of millions of dollars. And the cable, once laid, is expected to last at least twenty-five years.

Cables break.

This is one of the facts about the physical internet that people find most unsettling, and also most fascinating. The backbone of global communications, the system that carries trillions of dollars in financial transactions, billions of conversations, and the operational data of governments and militaries, is physically vulnerable. Cables get damaged. And when they do, someone has to go fix them.

The most common cause of cable damage is human activity, specifically, fishing trawls and ship anchors. A trawler dragging a net along the seabed in shallow water can snag a cable and tear it. A ship dropping anchor in the wrong place can cut through the armoring. These incidents account for roughly two-thirds of all cable failures. The remainder come from natural causes: undersea earthquakes, landslides, volcanic activity, and occasionally, though the threat is overstated in popular imagination, sharks. Sharks have been known to bite cables, possibly attracted by the electromagnetic fields, though modern cable armoring has largely eliminated this as a serious risk. The shark stories are irresistible, but anchors are the real villain.

When a cable breaks, the repair process is a remarkable operation in its own right. A specialized cable repair ship, there are only a few dozen in the world, sails to the approximate location of the break, identified by monitoring systems that can pinpoint the failure to within a few miles. The ship drags a grapnel along the seafloor to hook the cable and haul it to the surface. The damaged section is cut out, and a new section of cable is spliced in, a process that involves aligning glass fibers thinner than a human hair with microscopic precision, in the middle of the ocean, on a ship that's rolling in the swell. The repaired cable is then lowered back to the seabed.

A repair can take one to three weeks, depending on the depth, the weather, the location, and the availability of a repair ship. During that time, internet traffic that would normally flow through the damaged cable is rerouted through other cables, because the system is designed with exactly this kind of failure in mind. No single cable carries all of anyone's traffic. The network has redundancy built in, so that a break in one cable is an inconvenience for engineers, not a catastrophe for users. You've almost certainly had your data rerouted around a cable failure at some point, and you never noticed.

There are currently more than five hundred undersea cables in operation around the world, with new ones being planned and laid every year. If you could see them all at once, mapped onto the globe, they would look like a vast web, dense across the Atlantic and Pacific, branching through the Mediterranean and the South China Sea, reaching down to Africa, across to Australia, threading through the straits and channels that connect the world's oceans.

This map is not random. It reflects geography, economics, and history. The densest concentration of cables connects North America to Europe, the route of the heaviest internet traffic in the world, and the route that traces back to those first telegraph cables of the nineteenth century. The second densest concentration connects Asia to North America, reflecting the enormous growth in Pacific Rim data traffic over the past two decades. Africa, by contrast, has historically been underserved, fewer cables, less capacity, higher costs, though this is changing rapidly as new cables are laid along the African coast and across the Indian Ocean.

The geography of cables matters because it shapes the geography of the internet. Cities where many cables converge, places like New York, London, Marseille, Singapore, Tokyo, Mumbai, become internet hubs, with major data centers and network exchange points clustered nearby. The cables don't just carry data *through* these cities. They make these cities central to the internet's architecture. If you're standing in Marseille, you're standing at one of the most important intersections of the global internet, not because of any decision anyone made about Marseille specifically, but because that's where the cables from Africa, the Middle East, and Asia land on European soil.

. . .

This geography also creates vulnerabilities. A handful of chokepoints, narrow straits, shallow coastal zones, and landing station clusters, carry a disproportionate share of the world's internet traffic. The Strait of Malacca, the Suez Canal, the English Channel, the coast of Egypt: these are places where a natural disaster, a conflict, or even a careless anchor could disrupt communications for millions of people. The internet was designed to be decentralized, but the physical layer, the actual cables, concentrates in ways that the logical layer does not. Understanding this tension between the internet's decentralized architecture and its physically concentrated infrastructure is one of the things that separates informed observers of the digital world from casual users.

The ocean cables carry data between continents. But how does that data get from the cable landing station to your neighborhood, and from your neighborhood to your device?

This is the part of the internet's physical infrastructure that most people encounter without ever seeing. It's the network of cables, switches, and towers that connects the undersea backbone to your front door. Engineers break it into three layers: the backbone, the middle mile, and the last mile.

The backbone is the long-haul network: the undersea cables just discussed, plus the major terrestrial fiber routes that cross continents. In the United States, for example, thick bundles of fiber-optic cable run along highway corridors and railway rights-of-way, connecting major cities in a web of high-capacity links. These are the interstate highways of the internet. They carry enormous volumes of data over long distances at very high speeds, connecting the major hubs where internet traffic is exchanged and distributed.

The middle mile is the regional network that connects the backbone to local areas. Think of it as the state highways and county roads, the links between the interstate and your town. These are operated by regional internet service providers and telecommunications companies, and they bring high-speed connectivity from the major hubs to smaller cities, suburbs, and rural areas. The middle mile is less glamorous than the undersea cables, but it's just as essential. Without it, the backbone's capacity would have no way to reach the people who need it.

And then there's the last mile, the final stretch of network that connects the local infrastructure to your home, your office, or your device. This is the part of the internet you're most likely to interact with directly, and it's also the part with the most variation.

In some places, the last mile is fiber optic: glass cable running directly to your house, delivering data at extraordinary speed. In other places, it's copper, the old telephone lines, repurposed to carry internet data using technology that squeezes remarkable performance out of infrastructure that was designed for voice calls. In others, it's coaxial cable, the same kind used for cable television, shared among many households in a neighborhood. And in many places, especially rural areas and developing regions, the last mile is wireless: cellular towers broadcasting signals over the air, connecting phones and hotspots to the nearest wired network.

The last mile matters more than most people realize, because it shapes your experience of the internet in fundamental ways. You might live a few miles from a backbone hub with enormous capacity, but if the last mile to your house is an aging copper wire or a congested cellular tower, your internet will feel slow. The backbone is fast everywhere. The middle mile is usually adequate. But the last mile varies enormously, by neighborhood, by building, sometimes by floor, and it's the primary reason why some people have fast, reliable internet and others don't.

This variation isn't just an inconvenience. It's a form of inequality. Access to fast, affordable internet has become essential to modern life, for education, for work, for healthcare, for government services, for social participation. When the last mile fails or doesn't exist, people are locked out of systems that everyone else takes for granted. The inequality originates in the physical infrastructure: the cables, towers, and networks that do or don't reach your door. For readers whose interest extends into the civilisational impact of these systems, the fifth book in this series explores that digital divide in depth.

Now for the fundamental question at the heart of all of this: how does data physically travel?

You know the route now, from your device through the air to a local antenna, through cables to the local network, through the middle mile to the backbone, across undersea cables or long-haul terrestrial fiber, and into a data center on the other end. But what is actually moving through those cables? What is the physical substance of the internet?

In fiber-optic cables, the answer is light. A laser at one end of the fiber pulses on and off, billions of times per second, and each pulse represents a tiny piece of data. The light travels through the glass core of the fiber, bouncing off the inner walls at a precise angle, covering vast distances with remarkably little loss. At the other end, a sensor reads the pulses and reconstructs the data.

The idea of guiding light through a transparent medium is older than you might expect. In the 1840s, around the same time Cyrus Field was dreaming of his Atlantic cable, physicists demonstrated that light could be bent and guided through curved streams of water, following the curve rather than traveling in a straight line. The principle, called total internal reflection, means that light entering a transparent material at the right angle bounces off the inner surfaces rather than escaping, effectively trapping the light inside. It's the same principle that makes a diamond sparkle: light enters and bounces around inside rather than passing straight through.

. . .

For over a century, total internal reflection was a laboratory curiosity. The breakthrough that made fiber optics practical came in the 1960s and 1970s, when researchers figured out how to manufacture glass pure enough to carry light over long distances without it fading away. The purity required is staggering: a solid block of this glass a hundred miles thick would be as transparent as a windowpane. That purity is what allows light to travel through thousands of miles of fiber with enough clarity to be read at the other end. By the 1980s, fiber-optic cables were being laid in earnest, first on land, connecting cities and telephone exchanges, and then, inevitably, across ocean floors, following the paths that copper telegraph cables had pioneered a century before.

The speed is almost incomprehensible. Light in a fiber-optic cable travels at roughly two-thirds the speed of light in a vacuum, about 124,000 miles per second. A signal can cross the Atlantic Ocean in under 60 milliseconds. That's roughly the time it takes you to blink once. Your data, your message, your photo, your search query, is literally traveling as light, through a glass thread, at a speed that reduces continental distances to fractions of a second.

In copper cables, the mechanism is different, electrical signals rather than light, and the speed and capacity are lower. But the principle is the same: information encoded as a physical signal, traveling through a physical medium, from one point to another. And in wireless links, Wi-Fi, cellular, the data travels as radio waves through the air, at the full speed of light, until it reaches an antenna connected to the wired network.

. . .

Every piece of data you send or receive, no matter what it is, has a physical form. It exists as light in a glass thread, as electricity in a copper wire, or as a radio wave in the air. The internet is not abstract. It is as physical as a letter in the mail, just incomprehensibly faster.

Imagine, for a moment, that you could see the internet the way a bird sees highways. From high enough above, you'd see the undersea cables stretching across the ocean floors, thin lines of glass and steel connecting the continents, converging at landing stations on distant shores. You'd see the backbone fibers running along highways and railway corridors, carrying the data inland. You'd see the middle mile branching outward, reaching into suburbs and smaller cities. And you'd see the last mile, a tangle of fiber, copper, coaxial cable, and cellular towers, reaching down to individual homes, offices, schools, and phones.

The whole thing is a tree, rooted in the ocean and branching upward into every corner of human habitation. It carries light. It carries your life. And almost nobody sees it.

The next time you're walking down a street, look at the utility poles and the cables strung between them. Look at the manhole covers that provide access to underground conduits. Look at the cell towers disguised as trees or mounted on rooftops. Look at the small boxes on the side of buildings where fiber enters the premises. These are the visible traces of the internet, the physical infrastructure that carries your digital life.

The internet is not somewhere else. It's right here, all around you, hiding in plain sight.

Now let's go inside the buildings where all of this data arrives, is processed, and is sent back out again. Next, we step through the door of a data center, the factory of the digital age, and see what's inside: the racks, the servers, the cooling systems, the blinking lights, and the people who keep it all running.

CHAPTER 4

INSIDE A DATA CENTER: THE FACTORIES OF THE DIGITAL AGE

You've driven for forty minutes from the nearest city, past strip malls and subdivisions that thinned into farmland, then into a stretch of flat, quiet nothing, the kind of landscape where the biggest landmark is a water tower. You turn off the highway onto a two-lane road, follow it for a mile, and there it is: a long, low building set back behind a chain-link fence topped with barbed wire. The building is white or gray or beige, the color of something designed not to be noticed. There are no windows. No logos. No signs except a small placard with an address number. It could be a warehouse. It could be a distribution center for auto parts. It looks like a place where nothing interesting happens.

It is, in fact, one of the most important buildings in the modern world.

. . .

Behind that fence, past the security booth and the bollards designed to stop a truck, through a door that requires a badge and a biometric scan to open, a significant fraction of the digital life you lead every day is humming along: your photos, your messages, your searches, your transactions, the video you watched last night, the document you'll open tomorrow. This building and thousands like it, scattered across the globe in places most people will never see, are the physical heart of the cloud.

You know data centers exist. You know your data lives in them. Now let's go inside and see what's actually there.

The building you're about to enter is the latest chapter in a story that stretches back to the dawn of the computer age.

The first "data centers" weren't called data centers at all. They were called computer rooms, because they held a single computer, and that computer was large enough to fill a room. In the 1940s and 1950s, machines like ENIAC at the University of Pennsylvania occupied 1,800 square feet, weighed thirty tons, and used so much electricity that legend has it the lights in the surrounding neighborhood dimmed when it powered on. These machines required climate control, specialized power, raised floors for cabling, and restricted access, not because the designers were thinking about data center best practices, but because the machines were so expensive and so delicate that they had to be treated like patients in an intensive care unit.

. . .

Through the 1960s and 1970s, as mainframes became the backbone of corporate computing, the rooms that housed them grew more sophisticated. Companies built dedicated facilities: raised floors, redundant power, halon fire suppression systems, security guards. IBM published guidelines for computer room design that became informal industry standards. If you walked into a corporate computer room in 1975, you'd recognize many of the features you'll see in the data center we're about to tour: the raised floor, the cold air flowing upward through tiles, the racks of equipment, the hum of cooling systems. The scale was smaller. The principles were already in place.

The internet era of the 1990s changed the scale dramatically. Suddenly, companies needed servers, lots of them, to run websites and online services. The "server closet" became a common sight in office buildings: a repurposed room, often without proper cooling, crammed with machines balanced on folding tables, cables snaking across the floor, a portable air conditioner wheezing in the corner. These improvised setups worked for small operations, but they couldn't scale, and they couldn't deliver the reliability that businesses increasingly depended on.

That gap, between what companies needed and what a server closet could provide, gave birth to the modern data center industry. In the late 1990s and 2000s, specialized companies began building purpose-designed facilities: buildings engineered from the ground up for computing, with redundant power, industrial cooling, advanced fire suppression, and the physical security to match. When the cloud emerged in the mid-2000s, the hyperscale data center followed, facilities so large and so dense that they resemble nothing so much as the industrial factories of the nineteenth century, except that instead of producing steel or automobiles, they produce computation.

The building you're standing in front of right now is the descendant of all of these: the university computer room, the corporate mainframe hall, the improvised server closet, and the purpose-built facility. It has inherited their lessons, solved their problems, and scaled beyond anything their builders imagined.

Let's go inside.

The first thing you notice is the sound.

It hits you the moment you step through the inner door into the server hall, a low, continuous roar, like standing near a waterfall or inside the cabin of a plane at cruising altitude. It's the sound of thousands of fans spinning simultaneously, pulling cool air across circuit boards and pushing hot air out the other side. The sound never stops. It never changes pitch. It's the background hum of the digital world, and after a few minutes you stop noticing it, the same way you stop noticing the sound of an air conditioner. But it's there, always, filling the building from floor to ceiling.

. . .

The second thing you notice is the cold.

Data centers are kept cool, aggressively cool. The temperature in a server hall is typically maintained between 65 and 75 degrees Fahrenheit, and in some facilities the cold aisles, the rows where cool air is pushed in, feel closer to 60. If you walked in from a summer parking lot, you'd feel the temperature drop ten or fifteen degrees the moment the door closed behind you. This isn't for the comfort of the people who work here. It's for the machines. Servers generate heat, a lot of it, and if that heat isn't managed constantly, the machines will overheat, throttle their performance, and eventually fail. The entire cooling infrastructure of a data center exists to solve one problem: keeping the machines at the right temperature so they can keep running.

The third thing you notice is the light, or rather, the particular quality of it. Server halls are not brightly lit. The overhead lighting is functional, not inviting, enough to work by, not enough to read a book. But the servers themselves produce their own light: tiny LEDs on every machine, blinking green and amber and occasionally red, thousands of them in every direction. In a dark server hall, the effect is striking. Rows of metal cabinets stretching into the distance, each one studded with flickering points of light, like a city seen from an airplane at night. Each blinking light represents activity: a request being processed, data being written, a connection being maintained. The lights never go dark, because the machines never stop working.

Let's look more closely at what fills this building.

The basic unit of a data center is the server rack, a tall metal cabinet, usually about seven feet high and two feet wide, that holds servers stacked vertically like books on a shelf. A single rack might hold twenty, thirty, or forty individual servers, depending on their size and configuration. Each server is a flat metal box, think of a pizza box, roughly, that slides into the rack on rails. From the front, you see the face of each server: indicator lights, a small label, and the whir of internal fans. From the back, you see a tangle of cables, power cables, network cables, and fiber-optic connections, running to the overhead cable trays or the floor below.

A server, at its core, is just a computer. It has a processor (or several), memory, storage, and a network connection, the same basic components as the laptop on your desk or the phone in your pocket. The difference is in the optimization. Your laptop is designed for one person, doing many different things, in a form factor that fits in a bag. A server is designed for one thing, responding to requests from far away, and it does that one thing extraordinarily well. It doesn't need a screen, a keyboard, a touchpad, or speakers. It doesn't need to be portable or attractive. It needs to be fast, reliable, and efficient. Everything else has been stripped away.

The racks are arranged in long rows, dozens or hundreds of them, filling the floor of the building. And here's where the engineering gets clever: the rows are arranged in alternating pairs, one row facing one direction, the next row facing the other, to create a pattern of *hot aisles* and *cold aisles.*

Cold air is pushed up through perforated floor tiles (or blown in from overhead ducts) into the cold aisles, the spaces between the fronts of two facing rows of servers. The servers draw that cold air in through their front panels, across their internal components, and exhaust the heated air out the back, into the hot aisles, the spaces between the backs of two facing rows. The hot air rises and is captured by the cooling system, chilled, and recirculated. It's a continuous loop: cold air in the front, hot air out the back, captured, cooled, and pushed back in again.

This hot-aisle/cold-aisle arrangement is one of the most fundamental design principles in data center engineering, and it's been refined over decades. Without it, the cool air and warm air would mix randomly, making the cooling system far less efficient and the servers far harder to keep at the right temperature. The simple act of pointing the racks in alternating directions, and often sealing the aisles with doors or curtains to prevent air mixing, saves enormous amounts of energy and makes the difference between a facility that runs smoothly and one that runs hot.

Beneath your feet, there's more than meets the eye.

. . .

Many large data centers are built with raised floors. The surface you're walking on is actually a grid of removable tiles, elevated about two feet above the true concrete floor of the building. The space underneath, the *plenum*, is used as a massive air duct, distributing cool air from the cooling units to the perforated tiles in the cold aisles. It's also where much of the cabling runs: thick bundles of copper and fiber snaking between racks, connecting servers to switches, switches to routers, and routers to the outside world.

Above your head, cable trays carry additional runs of fiber and copper along the ceiling, like highways suspended in the air. Power distribution units hang from overhead racks or sit at the end of each row, converting the building's electrical feed into the precise voltages each server needs. Every rack has at least two independent power feeds, usually from entirely separate electrical paths, so that if one feed fails, the servers keep running on the other without interruption.

This redundancy is not an accident. It's a philosophy.

Redundancy is the single most important design principle in a data center, and you see it everywhere once you know to look.

Two power feeds to every rack, coming from different sources. Two (or more) network connections to the outside world, routed through different paths. Backup generators, usually massive diesel units sitting on concrete pads outside the building, that can take over the entire facility's electrical load within seconds if the grid power fails. Battery banks, rooms filled with industrial-scale uninterruptible power supplies, that keep the servers running during the ten to fifteen seconds it takes for the generators to spin up and stabilize. Redundant cooling systems, so that if one chiller fails, another picks up the load.

The principle behind all of this is simple: no single point of failure. Nothing in the building is so critical that its failure would bring the facility down. Every essential system has a backup, and most backups have backups of their own. Engineers describe this with a concept called "N+1": for every N components you need to run the facility, you build N plus one. Need three generators to power the building? Install four. Need two cooling units to keep the temperature stable? Install three. The extra unit sits idle most of the time, waiting for the moment it's needed. And when that moment comes, a generator fails during a heat wave, a cooling unit breaks at peak load, the backup engages seamlessly, and the facility keeps running as if nothing happened.

This is why the internet almost never goes down. Not because the equipment never fails; it does, regularly. The failures are absorbed by layers of redundancy that prevent any single failure from becoming visible to you. Your data is safe not because nothing ever goes wrong, but because the system is designed to keep working when things do go wrong. The foundation of that reliability starts here, in the physical design of the data center, and the full picture of how it holds together comes later.

Let's talk about the people.

You might spend an hour walking through a large data center and see only a handful of human beings. This isn't because the facility is unmanned; it's because the building is designed to run with minimal human intervention during normal operations. The servers are monitored remotely by software systems that track temperature, power consumption, network traffic, error rates, and hundreds of other metrics in real time. When something goes wrong, a drive failure, a temperature spike, a network anomaly, the monitoring system generates an alert, and a technician responds.

The technicians who work in data centers are a particular kind of professional. Their job is physical in a way that might surprise people who think of the internet as purely digital. They swap out failed hard drives, pulling the dead unit from its slot and clicking a replacement into place, sometimes dozens of times in a shift. They run cables, trace wiring faults, and replace power supplies. They walk the floor during rounds, checking for anything the monitoring systems might miss: a loose connection, a discolored LED, a subtle change in the sound of a fan that suggests a bearing is wearing out.

In the middle of the night, when a critical alert fires, a technician might drive to the facility from home, badge through security, walk to the affected rack, and spend an hour diagnosing and fixing a problem that, if left unaddressed, could cascade into something larger. By morning, the issue is resolved. A maintenance ticket is closed. And the millions of people whose data flows through that facility never knew anything was wrong.

There is something quietly heroic about this work. The entire digital world rests on the assumption that these buildings never stop, and they don't, because people make sure they don't. Behind the machines and the blinking lights, there are human beings who care about keeping this system running. The cloud is automated, but it is not unmaintained. Their stories, and the labor that sustains the digital world, come later in the series.

One question that people often ask when they first learn about data centers: why are they always in such strange locations?

You might expect the buildings that power the internet to be in major cities, close to the people who use them. Some are, especially smaller facilities that serve as local network hubs. But the massive hyperscale data centers, the ones run by the world's largest technology companies, the ones that contain hundreds of thousands of servers, tend to be in places that seem almost deliberately remote. Small towns in Oregon, Iowa, and Virginia. Rural Sweden. The outskirts of Dublin. The desert outside Las Vegas.

. . .

There are good reasons for this, and they all connect to the physical realities explored throughout these pages.

First, power. Data centers consume enormous amounts of electricity, and they need that electricity to be cheap, reliable, and ideally renewable. Rural areas near hydroelectric dams, wind farms, or nuclear plants offer abundant, affordable power that a city center often can't match. The full story of that energy consumption, and what it means, comes next.

Second, land. A hyperscale data center might cover a hundred thousand square feet or more, with room to expand. Urban real estate at that scale is expensive and scarce. Rural land is cheap and available.

Third, cooling. Data centers generate tremendous heat, and some locations offer natural advantages. Cool climates reduce the energy needed for air conditioning. Proximity to water sources can support evaporative cooling systems. Some facilities in northern Europe use the naturally cold outside air for much of the year, dramatically reducing their cooling costs.

Fourth, connectivity. This seems counterintuitive: why would a remote location have good internet connectivity? Because the data center operators bring it with them. They run dedicated high-capacity fiber connections from the facility to the nearest major network hub, often at their own expense. Once that fiber is in place, the facility can be as well-connected as any building in Manhattan. The physical distance doesn't matter much, because light in fiber-optic cable travels fast enough to make a hundred miles effectively instantaneous.

And fifth, risk distribution. If all of a company's data centers were in one city, a single earthquake, flood, or power grid failure could take them all down. Spreading facilities across multiple geographic regions, different states, different countries, different continents, ensures that no single disaster can affect everything at once.

So the next time you're driving through a quiet stretch of countryside and pass a large, windowless building surrounded by fences and cooling towers, give it a second look. There's a reasonable chance you're driving past the internet.

One thing to picture clearly, because it matters for everything that follows: the sheer scale of what's happening here.

The data center you've been touring is one facility. One building. And inside it, tens of thousands of servers are running simultaneously, each one handling thousands of requests per second, searches, messages, video streams, financial transactions, map queries, database operations, around the clock, every day, without stopping.

Now multiply that by thousands. There are thousands of data centers operating worldwide, ranging from small local facilities the size of a single room to hyperscale campuses with a dozen or more enormous buildings clustered together. The largest of these campuses cover millions of square feet and draw enough electricity to power a medium-sized city. Together, they form the physical foundation of the cloud, the global network of machines that stores, processes, and delivers the digital world.

This is not an abstraction. This is industry. These are real buildings, consuming real electricity, generating real heat, maintained by real people, built with real steel and concrete and fiber and silicon. The cloud is the largest industrial system most people have never thought about, and it's growing every year, driven by the same forces of demand and scale that shape every other industrial revolution.

But all of this, the machines, the racks, the cables, the buildings, requires one thing above all else to keep running: power. And power, in the world of data centers, is a story all its own.

What does it cost, in electricity and heat and water and environmental impact, to keep this machine running around the clock? The answer is both sobering and, in unexpected ways, inspiring.

CHAPTER 5

POWER AND HEAT: THE ENERGY BEHIND THE CLOUD

Every server in every rack in every data center you've just toured has one thing in common: it is hungry for electricity.

From the moment a server is switched on, it draws power, constantly, without pause, twenty-four hours a day, seven days a week, year after year. It draws power to run its processors. It draws power to spin its fans. It draws power to keep its memory active and its network connections alive. And every watt of electricity it consumes becomes a watt of heat, radiating off the circuit boards and into the surrounding air. Multiply that by tens of thousands of servers in a single building, and you begin to understand the fundamental challenge of running a data center: the electricity never stops flowing, and the heat never stops building.

The cloud, for all its ethereal name, is one of the most energy-intensive industries on the planet. And the scale of that energy consumption is something most people have never thought about, because the whole point of the cloud is that you don't have to think about it. You tap your phone. The answer appears. The electricity that made it happen is someone else's problem.

What follows is the story of that problem, and the extraordinary engineering that goes into solving it.

We've been here before.

In the late nineteenth century, as electrification transformed American industry, the relationship between power and progress was impossible to ignore. Factories that had once run on steam and water wheels were converting to electric motors, and in doing so, they were discovering that electricity wasn't just a better source of power. It was a different kind of problem. It had to be generated continuously, delivered reliably, and managed carefully. It produced heat as a byproduct. It required specialized infrastructure, generators, wiring, switchgear, safety systems, that was expensive to build and maintain. And the more a factory depended on it, the more catastrophic an outage became.

The parallels to modern data centers are striking. Just as an 1890s textile mill couldn't afford to have its electric motors stop mid-shift, a modern data center can't afford to have its servers go dark mid-transaction. Just as the factory needed backup systems for when the local generator failed, the data center needs backup systems for when the grid goes down. And just as the early electrification era was marked by a tension between the enormous benefits of electric power and the enormous costs of generating it reliably, the cloud era is marked by the same tension, scaled up to a global level.

The engineers who designed the first reliable electrical systems for factories, the redundant generators, the switchboards, the failover mechanisms, would recognize the engineering challenges inside a modern data center. The technology has changed. The principles haven't. Power must be continuous. Failure must be invisible. And the cost of keeping the machinery running is the price of everything the machinery makes possible.

Let's start with the numbers, because they're striking.

A single large data center can consume 30 to 50 megawatts of electricity, roughly the same as a small city of 25,000 to 40,000 homes. The biggest hyperscale campuses, with multiple buildings clustered together, can draw 100 megawatts or more. Globally, data centers consume somewhere between 1 and 2 percent of the world's total electricity production, and that figure is rising as demand for cloud services, streaming, and artificial intelligence continues to grow.

. . .

To put that in perspective: the electricity used by the world's data centers in a single year is comparable to the total electricity consumption of some mid-sized countries. This isn't a rounding error. It's a significant industrial footprint, on par with sectors like aluminum smelting or steel production, and it's growing faster than almost any other category of energy use.

The data center tour showed the machines, the racks, the cables. What it didn't show, because it happens mostly outside the building, is the infrastructure that keeps those machines fed with power. That infrastructure is enormous, and it begins at the point where the electrical grid meets the data center's front door.

Power enters a data center through dedicated high-voltage feeds, thick cables running from the local utility's substation to the facility's electrical room. Most large data centers have two or more independent feeds from the grid, routed through separate paths, so that a failure on one line doesn't take the building down. This is redundancy at the utility level, the same principle that governs every system inside the building, applied to the building's connection to the outside world.

Inside the electrical room, transformers step the voltage down from the high levels used for transmission to the lower levels the servers need. Switchgear directs power to different parts of the facility. Monitoring systems track every circuit, every load, every fluctuation. The electrical infrastructure of a large data center is as complex as that of a small industrial plant, because that's essentially what it is.

But the grid isn't always reliable. Storms knock out power lines. Equipment fails. Maintenance requires planned outages. A data center that depends entirely on the grid is a data center that will, eventually, go dark. And going dark, even for a few minutes, is unacceptable. The businesses and people who depend on these servers expect them to be available every second of every day. A five-minute outage at a major data center can cost millions of dollars, disrupt millions of users, and damage a company's reputation in ways that take years to repair.

So data centers don't depend entirely on the grid. They have their own backup power systems, and those systems are built to be virtually failproof.

The first line of defense is the uninterruptible power supply, the UPS.

A UPS is, at its simplest, a very large battery. In a data center, UPS systems are not the small boxes you might plug a desktop computer into at home. They're room-sized installations, banks of industrial batteries, sometimes filling an entire floor, connected to the facility's power distribution system. Their job is simple but critical: the moment grid power fails, the UPS takes over instantly, within milliseconds, keeping the servers running without so much as a flicker.

But batteries don't last forever. A UPS can sustain a data center's full load for somewhere between five and fifteen minutes, depending on the capacity of the battery banks and the power draw of the facility. That's not enough to ride out a major outage. It's enough to bridge the gap to the second line of defense: the generators.

Behind or beside most large data centers, sitting on reinforced concrete pads, you'll find a row of diesel generators, massive engines, each the size of a shipping container, capable of producing several megawatts of power. When the grid fails and the UPS kicks in, the generators start automatically. Within ten to fifteen seconds, they're running at full speed, producing enough electricity to power the entire facility. The UPS hands off the load to the generators, and the data center keeps running, now on its own power, independent of the grid, for as long as the diesel fuel holds out. Most facilities keep enough fuel on site to run for one to three days, with contracts in place for emergency fuel delivery if the outage lasts longer.

The generators are tested regularly, typically once a month, by running them under load to make sure they'll perform when needed. Some facilities conduct planned "pull tests," deliberately disconnecting from the grid to verify that the entire failover chain, grid to UPS to generator, works flawlessly from end to end. These tests are taken seriously, because the consequences of a failure in the backup chain are severe.

The result of all this layered protection is that a well-designed data center can survive almost any power disruption without its users ever knowing anything happened. The grid can fail, and the batteries catch it. The batteries buy time for the generators. The generators can run for days. And through it all, the servers keep humming, the data keeps flowing, and you keep scrolling, streaming, and searching without interruption.

But keeping the servers powered is only half the challenge. The other half is keeping them cool.

Remember the fundamental equation: every watt of electricity a server consumes becomes a watt of heat. A single server doesn't produce much, maybe a few hundred watts, comparable to a few incandescent light bulbs. But a rack of forty servers produces several kilowatts. A row of fifty racks produces hundreds of kilowatts. A server hall with thousands of racks produces megawatts of heat, continuously, without pause, day and night. If that heat isn't removed, the temperature inside the building would climb rapidly, and within minutes the servers would begin to overheat, throttle their performance, and eventually shut down.

Cooling is not a secondary concern in data center design. It is *the* concern: the single largest engineering challenge, the single largest operating cost after electricity, and the single largest driver of facility design decisions. The hot-aisle/cold-aisle arrangement you saw in the server hall is just the beginning. Behind it lies an elaborate system of cooling infrastructure that rivals the server infrastructure in complexity.

The challenge is as old as computing itself. ENIAC, the room-sized machine from the 1940s, generated so much heat that its operators sometimes opened the building's doors in winter and let the Philadelphia cold air flow through, because the primitive cooling systems couldn't keep up. The early main-frames of the 1950s and 1960s required dedicated air conditioning, a novelty in that era, just to keep their vacuum tubes from burning out. When transistors replaced vacuum tubes and then microchips replaced transistors, each generation produced less heat per component, but the number of components per machine grew so fast that the total heat output kept rising. The cooling problem has never gone away. It has only changed shape.

The most common approach today, and the one that has been standard for decades, is air cooling. Massive computer room air conditioning units, CRACs, in industry shorthand, sit at the edges of the server hall or in adjacent mechanical rooms. These units chill air and push it into the plenum beneath the raised floor, where it flows to the cold aisles and is drawn through the servers. The hot exhaust air rises, is captured by return ducts, and is piped back to the CRACs to be chilled again. The system runs continuously, circulating millions of cubic feet of air every hour in a never-ending cycle of cooling and heating.

• • •

Air cooling works, but it has limitations. Air is not a particularly efficient medium for absorbing heat. Moving enormous volumes of it requires powerful fans that consume significant energy. And as server densities increase, as more powerful processors generate more heat in the same physical space, air cooling struggles to keep up.

This is why the industry has been moving, steadily and sometimes dramatically, toward liquid cooling.

Liquid cooling comes in several forms. In the simplest version, chilled water circulates through pipes attached to heat exchangers mounted on or near the servers, absorbing heat far more efficiently than air can. In more advanced systems, coolant flows directly over the processors themselves, sometimes through sealed channels built into the server hardware, sometimes by submerging entire servers in tanks of non-conductive liquid that absorbs heat on contact. This sounds exotic, but it's becoming increasingly common, especially in facilities that run the high-powered processors used for artificial intelligence training, where heat generation per chip has outpaced what air can handle.

Other approaches push the boundaries further. Some companies have experimented with placing data centers underwater, sealed capsules on the ocean floor, cooled by the surrounding seawater. Others have built facilities in Arctic or subarctic climates, where the naturally cold outside air provides free cooling for most of the year. Still others capture the waste heat from their servers and pipe it into district heating systems, warming nearby homes and offices with the thermal byproduct of computing. In one Nordic city, a data center provides a meaningful fraction of the local district heating supply, turning a waste product into a community resource.

These innovations are driven by two forces: the relentless increase in computing density, which produces more heat per square foot, and the growing urgency of energy efficiency, which demands that less energy be spent on cooling and more on actual computing. The ideal data center would convert every watt of electricity into useful computation with zero waste. That's physically impossible; thermodynamics doesn't allow it. But the gap between ideal and actual is narrowing every year.

There is one more resource that data centers consume in quantities that surprise most people: water.

Many cooling systems, particularly the large evaporative cooling towers that sit outside data centers in warmer climates, use water as part of the heat rejection process. Water absorbs heat as it evaporates, and evaporative cooling is one of the most energy-efficient ways to dissipate the enormous thermal load a data center produces. But it requires a lot of water. A single large data center might consume hundreds of thousands of gallons per day during peak cooling periods, enough to be noticeable in regions where water is scarce.

. . .

This creates tension. Some of the places that are most attractive for data centers, sunny, arid regions with cheap land and abundant solar power, are also places where water is a precious and contested resource. Communities in the American Southwest, in parts of Australia, and in arid regions of the Middle East have raised legitimate concerns about data center water consumption competing with agricultural, residential, and environmental needs.

The industry is aware of this tension and is responding in several ways. Some operators have shifted to closed-loop cooling systems that recirculate water rather than evaporating it. Others have moved to air-cooled chillers that use no water at all, trading higher energy consumption for zero water usage. And some have designed facilities specifically for climates where natural cooling, cold outside air, eliminates the need for both water-intensive evaporative systems and energy-intensive mechanical chillers.

There is no perfect solution. Every cooling strategy involves tradeoffs between energy efficiency, water consumption, capital cost, and climate suitability. But the direction is clear: the industry is moving toward systems that use less water, less energy, and more ingenuity.

All of this, the electricity, the cooling, the water, the backup power, adds up to a significant environmental footprint. And it would be dishonest to pretend otherwise.

Data centers are responsible for a meaningful share of global electricity consumption, and electricity generation still relies heavily on fossil fuels in many parts of the world. The carbon footprint of the cloud is real. The water consumption is real. The land use is real. The electronic waste generated when servers reach the end of their useful life, typically three to five years, is real. These are not hypothetical concerns. They are measurable, documented, and growing.

But it would be equally dishonest to tell only that side of the story.

The cloud industry has become one of the largest private purchasers of renewable energy in the world. The major cloud operators have invested billions of dollars in solar farms, wind installations, and long-term power purchase agreements that bring new renewable capacity onto the grid. Some of the largest data center campuses are already powered entirely by renewable energy, or have committed to reaching that goal within the next few years. This isn't just public relations. It's economics: renewable energy, in many regions, is now the cheapest source of electricity available, and data center operators, who consume electricity at enormous scale, have every incentive to lock in the lowest rates.

. . .

Efficiency has improved dramatically as well. A metric called Power Usage Effectiveness, PUE, measures the ratio between total facility energy and the energy actually used for computing. A PUE of 2.0 means that for every watt powering a server, another watt is spent on cooling, lighting, and other overhead. A decade ago, a PUE of 2.0 was typical. Today, the most efficient hyperscale facilities achieve a PUE of 1.1 or even lower, meaning that nearly all the electricity entering the building goes directly to computation, with minimal waste.

Hardware efficiency has improved too. Modern servers deliver dramatically more computing power per watt than their predecessors. The amount of computation you can do with a kilowatt-hour of electricity has roughly doubled every two to three years for decades. This means that even as total data center energy consumption has grown, the amount of useful work done per unit of energy has grown faster. More streaming, more messaging, more searching, more storing, all with a smaller energy cost per transaction than ever before.

None of this means the problem is solved. The growth in demand, driven by streaming, cloud computing, and especially the enormous energy appetite of artificial intelligence, is outpacing efficiency gains in some categories. The industry is running faster, but the finish line is moving too. Sustainability in cloud computing is not a completed project. It's an active, ongoing engineering challenge, one that will require continued innovation in cooling technology, renewable energy deployment, hardware design, and responsible resource management.

The cloud has a physical cost. That's undeniable. It consumes electricity, generates heat, uses water, occupies land, and produces waste. These costs are real, and they deserve honest accounting, not hand-waving or greenwashing.

But the cloud also enables things that would be far more resource-intensive without it. Remote work reduces commuting and office energy consumption. Digital communication replaces physical mail and travel. Cloud-based logistics optimize shipping routes and reduce fuel waste. Shared computing infrastructure is vastly more efficient than the alternative: millions of companies each running their own servers in their own closets, with far worse utilization rates and far higher collective energy consumption.

The question isn't whether the cloud has an environmental cost. It does. The question is whether that cost is proportional to the value it creates, and whether the industry is making real progress in reducing it. On both counts, the honest answer is: it's complicated, it's imperfect, and it's improving.

Holding both the cost and the value in mind simultaneously, without flinching from either, is what it takes to evaluate the headlines, the claims, and the tradeoffs clearly. The cloud is not clean. But it's getting cleaner. And the engineers who designed the cooling systems, the power grids, and the renewable energy contracts are working on it with the same ingenuity that built the data centers, laid the cables, and created the infrastructure you've been exploring from the start.

Next comes a different question: not how the cloud stays powered, but how it stays *running*. The invisible engineering of reliability ensures the internet almost never goes down. What happens behind the scenes, on the rare occasions that it does, is a story of its own.

CHAPTER 6

RELIABILITY: WHY THE INTERNET ALMOST NEVER GOES DOWN

On a Monday afternoon, without any warning, one of the world's largest cloud platforms went dark.

It started with something small, a routine change to a network configuration, the kind of update that happens thousands of times a year without incident. But this time, the change contained an error. A single misconfiguration propagated through the system, and within minutes, services that hundreds of millions of people depended on began to fail. Social media platforms froze. Messaging apps stopped delivering messages. Businesses that ran their operations on the affected cloud infrastructure found their tools unresponsive. Customer support lines lit up. Headlines appeared within the hour.

The outage lasted several hours. Engineers worked through the night to identify the cause, reverse the change, and bring systems back online in a careful, staged sequence. By morning, the world had mostly moved on. A few jokes lingered on the platforms that had stayed up. A few opinion pieces questioned the fragility of the modern internet. And then everyone went back to using the cloud as if nothing had happened.

Here's the remarkable thing about that story: it made the news *because it was so unusual.*

We live in a world where billions of people use cloud-powered services every hour of every day, streaming, messaging, searching, paying, navigating, working, and the vast majority of the time, everything just works. The internet doesn't go down. Your email arrives. Your video plays. Your files are where you left them. The system operates with a reliability that we've come to take completely for granted, to the point where a few hours of disruption becomes a global news event.

That reliability is not an accident. It's not luck. It's the result of decades of engineering, designed from the ground up to ensure that failures, which happen constantly, at every level of the system, never become visible to you.

Here is how that works.

Let's start with a truth that might seem counterintuitive: things break all the time.

. . .

Inside a large data center, hardware failures are not rare events. They are daily occurrences. Hard drives fail. Memory chips develop errors. Network cables come loose. Fans wear out. Power supplies degrade. Software processes crash. At the scale of tens of thousands of machines running continuously, failure is not the exception; it's a statistical certainty. On any given day, in any large data center, something is broken or in the process of breaking.

If that sounds alarming, it shouldn't, because the entire system is designed around this reality. The engineers who build and operate cloud infrastructure don't try to prevent failure. They treat it as inevitable and design systems that keep working anyway.

This is the fundamental insight behind internet reliability: **the system doesn't work because nothing fails. It works because failures don't matter.**

This insight didn't originate in data centers. It was borrowed from industries where failure could kill people.

Aviation was one of the earliest fields to embrace the principle of designing for failure. In the 1930s and 1940s, as aircraft grew more complex and flew higher, engineers discovered that the question wasn't whether a component would fail; it was *when*.

A hydraulic line would eventually leak. An engine would eventually stall. An instrument would eventually give a false reading. The engineers couldn't prevent these failures. What they could do was ensure that no single failure brought the plane down. So they built redundancy into everything: two hydraulic systems, two electrical systems, multiple engines, backup instruments. If one system failed, the other carried the load. The philosophy was codified into a principle that the aviation industry still follows: no single point of failure.

The telephone network adopted the same philosophy. In the mid-twentieth century, as the phone system grew into a critical piece of national infrastructure, engineers at Bell Labs designed networks with multiple paths between any two points. If a cable was cut or a switching station failed, calls would route automatically through alternate paths. The user would never know anything had gone wrong. The principle was the same as aviation: assume failure will happen, and design the system to absorb it invisibly.

The internet inherited this thinking directly, because many of its early designers came from the telephone and defense industries, where failure-tolerant design was second nature. The principles at work here, redundancy, failover, monitoring, are not inventions of the cloud era. They're adaptations of ideas that have been refined for nearly a century, in industries where the stakes were as high as they come.

Once you understand them, you'll start to see them

everywhere, not just in data centers, but in any well-designed system that needs to stay running no matter what.

The first principle is redundancy, and you've already seen it in action.

The data center tour revealed a building where every critical system had a backup: two power feeds, two network connections, backup generators, battery banks, redundant cooling. The principle was simple: no single point of failure. If any one component fails, another takes over, and the system keeps running.

But redundancy in a single building only protects against local failures. What if the whole building goes down? What if a natural disaster, a flood, an earthquake, a wildfire, takes out an entire facility? What if the power grid in the region fails for days? What if a construction crew accidentally severs the fiber-optic cables connecting the building to the outside world?

This is where geographic distribution comes in.

Your data doesn't live in one data center. It lives in several, typically in different cities, often in different states or even different countries. When you store a photo in the cloud, the system doesn't put one copy in one building and hope for the best. It makes multiple copies and stores them in geographically separated locations. If one data center goes offline, for any reason, the other copies are still available, in buildings hundreds or thousands of miles away, completely unaffected by whatever happened at the first site.

This is called replication, and it happens automatically, behind the scenes, without any action on your part. You upload a photo. The system stores it in three places. You never know, and you never need to know. But if one of those places burns to the ground tomorrow, your photo is still safe in the other two.

The same principle applies to the services you use, not just the data they store. Major cloud-powered applications don't run in a single location. They run simultaneously in multiple regions, with traffic automatically distributed among them. If one region experiences a problem, the system shifts traffic to the others, often before anyone notices. The user experience remains smooth. The outage, if you can even call it that, is invisible.

The second principle is failover: the ability to switch from a failed system to a healthy one, automatically and almost instantly.

Imagine you're driving on a highway and the road ahead is suddenly blocked. In the physical world, you'd have to stop, wait for someone to clear the obstacle, or find an alternate route yourself. On the internet, the equivalent happens in milliseconds, without you doing anything.

When a server fails, the load balancer, the maître d' of the data center, detects the failure and stops sending requests to that machine. New requests are routed to other servers that are still healthy. The failed server is flagged for repair, and a technician will eventually replace the faulty component. But from the user's perspective, nothing happened. The request was answered. The page loaded. The message was delivered.

This automatic rerouting happens at every level of the system. If a network link between two routers goes down, traffic flows through an alternate path. If a fiber-optic cable is cut, data reroutes through another cable, sometimes across a different continent. If an entire data center loses connectivity, the services it was running continue in other locations. Each of these failover mechanisms is automatic, triggered by monitoring systems that detect failures within seconds and respond without waiting for a human to make a decision.

The speed of this response is critical. In the world of cloud infrastructure, a failure that's detected and remediated in five seconds is barely noticeable. A failure that takes five minutes to address might cause visible disruption. A failure that takes five hours is a headline. The entire monitoring and failover apparatus is built to keep response times as close to zero as possible, because in a system serving hundreds of millions of people, even a brief delay is felt by millions.

The third principle is monitoring: constant, automated, comprehensive surveillance of every component in the system.

A large cloud operation monitors thousands of metrics in real time: server health, network latency, error rates, disk usage, memory consumption, request volume, response times, temperature, power draw, and hundreds more. These metrics are collected continuously from every machine, every network link, every service, and fed into monitoring systems that watch for anomalies.

Think of it as a hospital's intensive care unit for machines. Every patient is connected to monitors that track heart rate, blood pressure, oxygen levels, and a dozen other vital signs. If any measurement moves outside the normal range, an alarm goes off and a specialist responds. Data center monitoring works the same way, except the patients are servers, the vital signs are digital metrics, and the specialists are engineers who can often diagnose and fix a problem without ever leaving their desk.

When something goes wrong, a server's response time spikes, a disk is approaching capacity, a network link is dropping packets, the monitoring system generates an alert. Minor issues might be handled automatically: a process is restarted, a workload is shifted, a backup system is activated. More serious issues trigger a page to an on-call engineer, who investigates, diagnoses, and resolves the problem, often in the middle of the night.

This monitoring never stops. It runs twenty-four hours a day, seven days a week, across every facility, every service, every machine. It's the nervous system of the cloud, constantly sensing, constantly reporting, constantly ensuring that problems are caught before they cascade.

These three principles, redundancy, failover, and monitoring, work together to create something that feels, from the outside, like perfection. The internet just works. Your files are always there. Your services are always available. It feels bulletproof.

But it isn't. And it's important to understand why.

Despite all the engineering, outages still happen. Not often, but they do, and when they affect major services, they're felt by millions of people simultaneously. Understanding why outages occur, even with all these safeguards in place, is part of understanding the system honestly.

The most common cause of significant outages is not hardware failure. Hardware failures happen constantly, and the system is designed to absorb them. The most common cause is *software*, specifically, bugs in the code that operates the infrastructure, or errors in the configurations that control how traffic flows, how data is stored, and how services communicate with each other.

The outage that opened this chapter was caused by a configuration error, a single incorrect change that cascaded through the system in ways that the engineers didn't anticipate. This kind of failure is particularly dangerous because it can bypass the physical redundancy that protects against hardware problems. If a misconfiguration tells the system to route all traffic to a nonexistent location, having three backup data centers doesn't help, because the instructions themselves are wrong.

Another common cause is cascading failure, a situation where one small problem triggers a chain of increasingly severe problems. A server goes down, and the traffic it was handling is redirected to other servers. Those servers are now under heavier load, which causes some of them to slow down or fail, which redirects even more traffic to the remaining healthy servers, which pushes them past their limits. Within minutes, a single server failure has become a system-wide overload. Engineers sometimes describe this as a "thundering herd," a surge of demand that overwhelms the system not because of any single fault, but because of the collective response to the initial failure.

And sometimes, the cause is simply the limits of human foresight. Complex systems interact in ways that no one can fully predict. Engineers design for every failure they can imagine, but occasionally the real world produces a failure they didn't imagine, a combination of circumstances so unlikely that no one thought to test for it. These are the failures that produce the most dramatic outages and the most useful lessons.

When a significant outage does occur, what happens next is as carefully engineered as the systems that prevented it from happening sooner.

The first priority is restoration, getting the service back online as quickly as possible. This typically involves identifying the failing component, isolating it from the rest of the system, and either fixing the problem or routing around it. In many cases, this means rolling back a recent change, reverting to the previous configuration or software version that was working correctly. Speed matters enormously. Every minute of downtime affects millions of users and can cost significant money.

Once the service is restored, the second priority is understanding. Cloud operations teams conduct post-incident reviews, sometimes called "post-mortems," that are among the most valuable practices in the industry. The goal is not to assign blame but to understand exactly what happened, why the safeguards didn't prevent it, and what can be done to ensure it doesn't happen again.

. . .

This practice, too, was borrowed from other industries. Aviation pioneered the blameless accident investigation, the principle that understanding *what went wrong* matters more than punishing *who* got it wrong, because blame discourages honesty, and without honesty, you can't learn. The National Transportation Safety Board, established in the 1960s, made this principle the foundation of air crash investigation: every detail is documented, every contributing factor is analyzed, and the findings are published openly so the entire industry can learn. The result, over decades, was a dramatic reduction in aviation fatalities, not because planes stopped having mechanical failures, but because every failure made every future flight safer.

Cloud operations adopted this model almost wholesale. The best post-mortems are unflinching in their honesty: they trace the chain of events from root cause to user impact, identify every point where the problem could have been caught earlier, and produce concrete action items to strengthen the system.

This culture of learning from failure is one of the most important, and least visible, reasons the internet is as reliable as it is. Every outage makes the system stronger, because every outage teaches the engineers something they didn't know before. The reliability you experience today was built on the failures of yesterday.

There's one more dimension of reliability that connects to

something you feel in your own life: the difference between the system going down and the system being slow.

Most people think of an outage as a binary event: the service works, or it doesn't. But in reality, the most common form of degradation is partial. The service still works, but it's slower, or some features are unavailable, or some users are affected while others aren't. You might notice that a page takes a few extra seconds to load, or that a video buffers briefly, or that a search returns results more slowly than usual. This is the system under stress, not failing, but straining.

These partial degradations are often managed deliberately by the engineers. When a system is under heavy load or experiencing a partial failure, the operations team may choose to disable non-essential features to protect the core experience. A streaming service might temporarily reduce video quality to avoid buffering. A social media platform might delay notification delivery to preserve the feed. An email service might slow down search functionality to keep message delivery running at full speed.

This is called graceful degradation, and it's a design philosophy that acknowledges reality: it's better to give users a slightly reduced experience than to give them no experience at all. The goal is always to protect the most important functions, the ones users depend on most, even if less critical features have to be temporarily sacrificed.

. . .

If you've ever noticed a service feeling slightly "off" without being completely broken, you may have been experiencing graceful degradation in action. The system was bending so it wouldn't break.

The internet feels like it always works because an enormous amount of engineering, physical, digital, and organizational, is dedicated to making sure it does. Redundancy at every layer. Automatic failover in milliseconds. Continuous monitoring of every component. Geographic distribution across continents. And a culture that treats every failure as an opportunity to learn and improve.

None of this is visible to you. When you tap your phone and get a response in half a second, you don't see the backup generators, the replicated data, the load balancers, the monitoring dashboards, or the engineer who fixed a disk failure at 3 AM so you'd never notice. You just see a result on your screen. It feels effortless because an extraordinary amount of effort went into making it feel that way.

But it's not perfect. It can't be. Complex systems fail in complex ways, and no amount of engineering can eliminate all risk. What the engineering can do, and does, remarkably well, is make failures rare, brief, and invisible to the vast majority of users, the vast majority of the time.

. . .

The next time a major service goes down and the headlines call it a "catastrophe," remember the context: it's news precisely because it almost never happens. The real story isn't the outage. The real story is the thousands of days between outages, the invisible, ongoing, relentless work that keeps the whole thing running.

Now for a question that's closer to home: where is *your stuff*? Your photos, your documents, your messages, your memories, they're somewhere in this vast machine. The next step is finding out exactly where, and how they're being kept safe.

CHAPTER 7

HOW YOUR STUFF LIVES IN THE CLOUD

Think about a photograph you care about.

Maybe it's from a wedding, or a vacation, or a birthday party. Maybe it's a picture of someone you love, taken on a random Tuesday, that turned out to be one of your favorites. You took it on your phone. You looked at it once or twice, maybe shared it with a few people. And then you moved on with your day.

That photo is still somewhere. Right now, as you read this, it exists, not as a memory in your mind, but as a physical object in the real world. It is sitting on a hard drive, in a server, in a rack, in a data center, in a building you've never visited, in a place you'd probably never think to look. It is stored as a pattern of magnetic charges or electrical states on a piece of hardware that hums quietly alongside tens of thousands of other pieces of hardware, all holding other people's photos, documents, messages, and memories.

. . .

Your photo has a location. It has neighbors. It is consuming a tiny amount of electricity right now, just by existing. And there's a very good chance that it exists not in one place, but in three, copied automatically to data centers in different cities, maybe different countries, so that if anything happens to one copy, the others survive.

Here is where your stuff actually lives, and how it's kept safe.

Let's start with what happens the moment you take that photo.

When you tap the shutter button on your phone's camera, the image is captured by the sensor, processed by the phone's software, and saved to your device's internal storage. At this point, it exists in exactly one place: the chip inside your phone. If you dropped your phone in a river right now, the photo would be gone.

But most phones today are configured to back up photos to the cloud automatically. Within seconds or minutes of taking the photo, depending on your connection and your settings, your phone uploads a copy to a cloud storage service. The photo travels from your device, through the local network, across the internet, and into a data center, where it's written to a storage system and associated with your account.

. . .

Now the photo exists in two places: your phone and the cloud. Drop the phone in a river, and the photo survives. You can open your laptop, log into the same account, and there it is, the same image, waiting for you on a completely different device.

This feels like magic. It isn't. It's the same round-trip journey, happening in the background while you go about your day.

But what does "stored in the cloud" actually mean? Where, physically, is the photo sitting?

The answer involves a system that is elegantly simple in concept and remarkably sophisticated in execution.

When your photo arrives at the cloud storage service, it isn't saved as a single file on a single hard drive. Instead, it's broken into pieces, chunks of data, each one a fragment of the original image. These chunks are then distributed across multiple storage devices, often across multiple machines, sometimes across multiple data centers. A metadata system, think of it as a master index, keeps track of which chunks belong to which file, where each chunk is stored, and how to reassemble them when you want to see the photo again.

Why break a file into pieces? Two reasons.

. . .

The first is performance. If a hundred thousand people are all trying to access their files at the same time, spreading the data across many machines means no single machine becomes a bottleneck. Different users' files are served by different storage devices, and even a single large file can be reassembled from chunks served simultaneously by multiple machines. The system can handle enormous volumes of requests without slowing down.

The second reason is durability. Each chunk isn't stored once; it's stored multiple times, on different machines, in different locations. This is the same principle of redundancy that protects the data center's power and cooling, applied to your data. If a hard drive fails, and hard drives fail constantly, as a simple matter of mechanical reality, the chunks stored on that drive still exist on other drives. The system detects the failure, notes which chunks were affected, and automatically creates new copies on healthy machines to restore the redundancy level. This happens without anyone asking for it, without anyone being notified, and without your photo being unavailable for even a moment.

The analogy that works best here is a library system with many branches. Imagine a library that keeps three copies of every book, each in a different building across the city. If one building floods, the book isn't lost; it's still available at the other two locations. And as soon as the flood is cleaned up, the library prints a new copy to replace the damaged one. The cloud works the same way with your data. Multiple copies, multiple locations, automatic replacement when a copy is lost.

The result is a level of durability that borders on the absurd. Major cloud storage providers engineer their systems to provide what's sometimes described as "eleven nines" of durability: 99.999999999 percent. That means if you stored ten million files, you could statistically expect to lose one file every ten thousand years. Your photo is safer in the cloud than it is on any single device you own, including the phone you took it on.

There's a word that keeps coming up in conversations about cloud storage, and it deserves a clear explanation: encryption.

Encryption is the process of scrambling data so that only authorized parties can read it. When your photo travels from your phone to the cloud, it's encrypted *in transit*, transformed into an unreadable jumble that can only be decoded by the server at the other end. Anyone who intercepted the data along the way, on the coffee shop's Wi-Fi, at a network router, anywhere in between, would see only gibberish.

Once the photo arrives at the data center and is stored on a disk, it's often encrypted again, this time *at rest*. The data on the physical storage device is scrambled, so that even if someone physically stole the hard drive, which, given the security infrastructure surrounding these facilities, would be extraordinarily difficult, they couldn't read what was on it without the encryption key.

For readers whose interest extends into the full architecture of cloud security and encryption, the third book in this series explores it in depth. For now, what matters is the principle: your data isn't just stored in the cloud. It's stored in a way that's designed to be unreadable to anyone who isn't supposed to see it, both while it's traveling and while it's sitting still.

One of the things that makes cloud storage feel almost magical is syncing: the ability to make a change on one device and see it appear on another, almost instantly.

You edit a document on your laptop. You close the laptop and pick up your phone. The document is already there, with your latest changes. You didn't email it to yourself. You didn't copy it to a thumb drive. It just appeared.

Here's how it works. When you edit a document that's stored in the cloud, your device sends the changes to the cloud server. The server updates its copy, the master copy, the single source of truth. Then the server notifies your other devices that the file has changed. Those devices download the updated version, and now all your devices have the same file, with the same changes.

. . .

The cloud is the middleman. It's the central point that all your devices check against. Your laptop doesn't talk to your phone directly. They both talk to the cloud, and the cloud keeps them in agreement. This is why syncing works across any number of devices, two, five, ten, and why it works even if some of your devices are turned off when the change is made. The next time a device comes online, it checks with the cloud and catches up.

This single-source-of-truth model is what makes the modern multi-device life possible. You can start a task on your computer at work, continue it on your tablet during your commute, and finish it on your phone at home, and the cloud ensures that you're always working on the same version of the same file. It's the invisible coordinator that makes the experience feel seamless.

It also explains why things occasionally go wrong. If two devices make changes to the same file at the same time, the cloud has to decide which version to keep, or, more commonly, it saves both and asks you to resolve the conflict. This is rare, but when it happens, it's a reminder that syncing isn't magic. It's a system, with rules, doing its best to keep everything in order.

Here's a question that nags at people once they start thinking about cloud storage: does the cloud ever run out of space?

. . .

The short answer is no, or at least, not in any way you'd notice.

Cloud storage providers manage enormous pools of capacity, measured in exabytes, where a single exabyte is a billion gigabytes. As users upload more data, the providers add more storage hardware, more drives, more racks, more data centers. The system is designed to grow ahead of demand, so that there's always capacity available when you need it.

From your perspective, cloud storage feels infinite. You never get a message saying "the cloud is full." You just keep uploading photos, saving documents, and sending messages, and the space is always there. This isn't because the storage is limitless; it's because the system is managed so that the limits are never reached before new capacity is added.

This is another expression of the elastic scale at the heart of the cloud, its ability to expand and contract based on demand. For storage, the expansion is mostly in one direction: up. The world produces more data every year than the year before, and the cloud grows to accommodate it.

There's one more topic that matters here, and it's the one most people prefer not to think about: what happens when your data goes away.

. . .

Deletion in the cloud is more complicated than you might expect.

When you delete a photo from your phone, it might still exist in the cloud, in your backup, in your cloud photo library, in a shared album, or in a trash folder that retains deleted items for a set period. Cloud services often keep deleted files for thirty, sixty, or ninety days before permanently removing them, specifically to protect you from accidental deletion. This is a feature, not a bug, but it means that "deleted" and "gone" are not always the same thing.

When a file is permanently deleted from the cloud, after the retention period expires, or when you explicitly empty the trash, the storage system marks the space as available for reuse. The actual data might linger on the disk for some time before being overwritten by new data, but it's no longer associated with your account and is no longer accessible through any normal means. For most practical purposes, it's gone.

But there's a broader version of this question worth considering: what happens to your data when you stop using a service entirely?

If you cancel a cloud storage subscription, the provider will typically retain your data for a grace period, a few weeks to a few months, before deleting it. If the provider itself shuts down, a smaller service going out of business, a company discontinuing a product, your data is at risk unless you've downloaded a copy before the shutdown. This has happened before, and it will happen again. Major providers are unlikely to vanish overnight, but smaller services do, and the lesson is clear: the cloud is an excellent place to store your data, but it's not a substitute for having your own copy of the things that matter most.

The safest approach is the simplest one: keep a copy of anything irreplaceable. Cloud storage is remarkably durable, but the combination of cloud backup *and* a local copy, on an external hard drive, for instance, gives you the best of both worlds. The cloud protects you from a broken phone. The local copy protects you from a broken cloud.

Your photo, the one from the wedding or the vacation or the random Tuesday, is not floating in an abstract digital space. It is sitting on a physical disk, in a physical machine, in a physical building, connected to a physical power supply and cooled by a physical cooling system. It exists as a pattern of electrical charges that represent a series of numbers that represent the colors of every pixel in the image. It has been broken into chunks, distributed across machines, replicated across data centers, encrypted at rest, and indexed by a metadata system that can locate and reassemble it in milliseconds.

Pause for a moment to appreciate how extraordinary this is, not just technically, but historically.

. . .

For most of human history, preserving a memory meant preserving a physical object. A painting on a cave wall. A scroll in a library. A letter in a drawer. Each one existed in exactly one place, and if that place was destroyed, the memory was gone. The Library of Alexandria burned, and centuries of accumulated knowledge vanished. Family letters were lost in floods. Diaries were discarded by heirs who didn't know what they contained.

Photography changed the equation, but only slightly. A photograph was still a physical object: a print, a negative, a slide. You could make copies, but each copy was another physical thing that had to be stored, maintained, and protected. Photographs faded in sunlight. Negatives degraded in damp basements. Shoeboxes of prints were thrown away during moves. The physical fragility of photographs meant that every family's visual history was perpetually at risk, one fire, one flood, one careless decision away from disappearing.

The digital era seemed to solve this. You could store photographs as files, sequences of numbers that didn't fade or degrade. But digital files introduced their own fragility. A hard drive could fail. A CD-ROM could scratch. A computer could crash. If you didn't make backups, and most people didn't, your digital photos were just as vulnerable as the prints they replaced. They lasted until the hardware broke, and then they were gone.

The cloud is the first storage system in human history that is durable at a personal scale. Your photo exists in three places at once, guarded by redundancy, monitored by automated systems, backed up automatically, encrypted, and available on any device you pick up. The eleven nines of durability, one lost file in ten million, every ten thousand years, represents a level of preservation that no library, no archive, no vault in human history has ever achieved for ordinary people's personal possessions.

A hundred years ago, a family's photographs were a single shoebox in a closet. Today, they're distributed across data centers on multiple continents, replicated automatically, and accessible from anywhere in the world. The human desire to preserve memories hasn't changed. The ability to do so has been transformed beyond recognition.

That's where your stuff lives. Not in the air. Not in the ether. In buildings, on machines, protected by engineering and maintained by people.

The next time you open your phone and scroll through your photos, you're looking at a window into a data center, a view into a building you've never seen, at a machine you'll never touch, in a place you'll probably never visit. But now you know it's there. You know what it looks like. And you know that your memories, your documents, and your digital life are being kept safe by the same infrastructure you've been exploring from the start.

. . .

Now it's time to zoom out and ask a bigger question: how does this system serve not just you, but the entire world at once? The concept that makes the cloud truly transformative is scale, and the way the cloud handles billions of requests simultaneously, expanding and contracting like a living thing, is the next piece of the picture.

CHAPTER 8

SCALE: HOW THE CLOUD HANDLES THE WHOLE WORLD AT ONCE

On a Sunday evening in the middle of summer, a billion-dollar sporting event reaches its final minutes. Hundreds of millions of people, on every continent, are watching the same game at the same time. They're streaming it on phones, tablets, laptops, and televisions, each one receiving a unique video feed, tailored to their device, their connection speed, their language, and their location. Millions more are refreshing live score apps, posting reactions on social media, sending messages to friends, and placing last-second bets. The traffic hitting the world's cloud infrastructure spikes to levels that would be staggering on a normal day.

And it all works.

No buffering for most viewers. No crashed apps. No frozen feeds. The systems that were handling ordinary Sunday traffic an hour ago are now handling a global surge, and they absorbed it without breaking, without slowing down in any visible way, and without anyone behind the scenes pressing a panic button.

How?

The answer is scale, specifically, a kind of scale that didn't exist before the cloud, and that remains one of the most quietly revolutionary concepts in modern computing. The cloud doesn't just handle a lot of traffic. It *grows* to handle more traffic, automatically, in real time, and shrinks back when the demand subsides. It breathes. It flexes. It expands to meet the moment and contracts when the moment passes.

This is the concept that makes the cloud transformative, not just big, but elastic. And once you understand it, you'll understand why the digital world feels so effortless, even when billions of people are using it at the same time.

To appreciate why elastic scale matters, it helps to understand the problem it solved, because it's a problem that's much older than the internet.

Every system that serves the public has peak moments, surges of demand that dwarf the ordinary load. The telephone network discovered this early. On Christmas Day and Mother's Day, call volumes spiked so dramatically that the system couldn't handle them all. Callers heard busy signals. Connections failed. The network was designed for an average day, and holidays overwhelmed it. The phone companies' solution was to overbuild, adding enough capacity to handle the peaks, but even then, the busiest hours of the busiest days routinely exceeded what the network could carry. For decades, "all circuits are busy" was a familiar frustration on holidays, and the phone companies simply accepted it as an unsolvable problem.

Retail had the same challenge in physical form. Department stores built for an average shopping day were overrun on Black Friday. Parking lots filled. Checkout lines stretched to the back of the store. Inventory ran out. The stores couldn't magically expand to accommodate the rush and then shrink back to normal size on Saturday morning. They were stuck with the building they had.

The early internet inherited this same rigidity.

Before the cloud, if you ran a website or an online service, you owned your servers. You bought physical machines, installed them in a room or a rented facility, and that was your capacity. If your website could handle ten thousand visitors at a time, that was your ceiling. If eleven thousand showed up, the site slowed down. If a hundred thousand showed up, because a news article went viral, or a product launch exceeded expectations, or a holiday shopping rush hit harder than predicted, the site crashed.

. . .

This created an impossible planning problem. You had to guess your peak demand, the busiest moment of your busiest day, and buy enough servers to handle it. But peak demand might happen a few days a year. The rest of the time, most of those servers sat idle, consuming electricity and generating heat while doing nothing useful. You were paying for capacity you almost never used, just to survive the rare moments when you needed all of it.

It was like building a ten-lane highway to handle rush-hour traffic, knowing that for twenty-two hours a day, eight of those lanes would sit empty.

Small companies couldn't afford this kind of overprovisioning, so they accepted the risk of crashing during surges. Large companies could afford it, but the waste was enormous. Either way, the system was rigid. You bought your capacity in advance, and you were stuck with it: too much on quiet days, too little on busy ones.

The cloud eliminated this problem entirely.

In a cloud-based system, you don't buy servers. You rent computing power from a provider that operates enormous pools of machines, the data centers you've already toured. When your service needs more capacity, the cloud allocates more machines to your workload. When the demand drops, those machines are released back to the pool, available for someone else to use. You pay for what you use, when you use it, and nothing more.

This is elasticity: the ability to grow and shrink on demand, automatically, in real time.

The best analogy I've found for this is a restaurant that can change its size.

Imagine a restaurant where, when a crowd arrives, the building instantly adds more tables, more chairs, more kitchens, and more waitstaff. The service stays smooth. Every customer gets seated. Every order is taken promptly. And when the crowd leaves, the extra tables and kitchens fold away, the staff clocks out, and the restaurant returns to its normal size, no wasted space, no idle employees, no overhead.

No physical restaurant can do this. But the cloud does it with computing power, every second of every day.

When a streaming service launches a highly anticipated show at midnight and millions of people hit play simultaneously, the cloud spins up thousands of additional servers to handle the surge. When the premiere rush subsides a few hours later, those servers are released. When a retail site experiences a Black Friday traffic spike ten times its normal volume, the cloud stretches to accommodate it and contracts when the sales end. When a small startup's app unexpectedly goes viral and traffic jumps from a thousand users to a million in a single afternoon, the cloud scales up to meet the demand without the startup buying a single piece of hardware.

This is why modern digital experiences feel effortless even at enormous scale. The infrastructure behind them is not a fixed resource waiting to be overwhelmed. It's a fluid, responsive system that adapts to demand in real time.

But elasticity alone isn't enough to explain why you can stream a video from the other side of the world without buffering, or why a search engine can return results in a fraction of a second no matter where you are. There's another piece of the puzzle: bringing the content closer to you.

This is where content delivery networks, CDNs, come in.

Think about what happens when a new episode of a popular show drops on a streaming platform. Millions of people, spread across dozens of countries, want to watch it at the same time. If every one of them had to fetch the video from a single data center, say, in Virginia, the cables, routers, and servers between Virginia and a viewer in Tokyo or São Paulo or Lagos would be overwhelmed. The distance alone would introduce noticeable delay. The volume would make it worse.

. . .

So the streaming platform doesn't serve the video from one location. It copies the video, in advance, to servers positioned all around the world, in dozens or hundreds of cities. When you press play, you're not getting the video from Virginia. You're getting it from a server in your city, or at least in your region. The content has been placed close to you before you even asked for it.

This is a CDN: a network of servers, distributed geographically, that cache popular content near the users who want it. Think of it as the difference between a central archive and a system of local branch libraries. You don't travel to the national library every time you want a book. You go to the branch down the street, where the most popular titles are already on the shelf. If the branch doesn't have what you're looking for, it can request it from the central collection, but most of the time, it's already there.

CDNs are one of the reasons the internet feels fast everywhere, not just in the cities where the big data centers are. They reduce the distance your data has to travel, which reduces the time it takes to arrive, which makes the experience feel instant. When you watch a video without buffering, thank a CDN server that's probably sitting in a building less than fifty miles from where you are right now.

There's a third mechanism that operates alongside elasticity and CDNs, and it's one you've already encountered: load balancing.

. . .

The load balancer, the maître d' who distributes incoming requests across multiple servers so that no single machine gets overwhelmed, becomes even more critical and more sophisticated at this scale.

When hundreds of millions of people are using a service simultaneously, the load balancer isn't just distributing requests across servers in one data center. It's distributing them across multiple data centers, in multiple regions, on multiple continents. A user in London might be served by a data center in Dublin. A user in Tokyo might be served by a data center in Singapore. A user in New York might be served by a data center in Virginia. The load balancer, or, more accurately, a hierarchy of load balancers working together, ensures that each request goes to the server that can respond the fastest, based on geographic proximity, current load, and available capacity.

This is called global load balancing, and it's what allows a single service to feel local to everyone, everywhere, simultaneously. When you use a search engine or a social media platform, you're not connecting to "the" server. You're connecting to one of thousands of servers, in one of dozens of locations, selected for you in milliseconds based on where you are and which machine is best positioned to help you right now.

The combination of these three mechanisms, elastic scaling, content delivery networks, and global load balancing, is what makes the modern cloud capable of serving the entire world at once. Each one is conceptually simple. Together, they produce something that feels miraculous: a system that handles billions of requests per day, from every country on Earth, without breaking a sweat.

There's a human dimension to scale that's easy to lose in the mechanics.

Scale is the reason you have the digital life you have.

Before the cloud made elastic scale possible, building a global digital service required enormous upfront investment. You needed your own data centers, your own servers, your own networking infrastructure, and you needed enough of it to handle your peak demand from day one. Only the largest companies in the world could afford to build at that scale. The barrier to entry was measured in hundreds of millions of dollars.

The cloud lowered that barrier to nearly zero. Today, a college student with a laptop and a credit card can launch an app that serves millions of users worldwide. They don't buy servers. They don't lease data center space. They don't hire operations staff. They rent capacity from the cloud, starting with almost nothing and scaling up only as demand grows. If the app fails, they've spent almost nothing. If it succeeds, the infrastructure grows with them automatically.

. . .

This is why the app economy exploded in the past fifteen years. It's why a startup founded in a dorm room can reach a hundred million users within months. It's why services that serve the entire planet can be built by small teams. The cloud's elastic scale didn't just make existing services faster or cheaper. It made entirely new kinds of services *possible*, services that never could have existed in a world where you had to buy your infrastructure before you had a single customer.

The streaming service you watch, the messaging app you use, the maps you navigate with, the social media you scroll: many of these were built by small teams that grew into global services on the back of cloud infrastructure. Scale is the invisible engine that powers the modern digital economy.

There is, however, a tension inside the story of scale that deserves honest acknowledgment.

The same elastic infrastructure that enables a student to launch a global app also enables the largest companies in the world to operate at a scale that no competitor can match. The economics of cloud infrastructure favor size: the bigger the provider, the cheaper each unit of computing becomes, and the better the service for users. This creates a gravitational pull toward concentration, a small number of very large providers serving the majority of the world's cloud needs.

. . .

Notice the pattern: scale is the cloud's greatest strength, and it naturally favors the large over the small. The same force that enables innovation also enables dominance. Both are true at the same time. For readers whose interest extends into what that concentration means for power, governance, and the structure of digital society, the fifth book in this series explores it in depth.

A thought experiment puts all of this into perspective.

Imagine it's New Year's Eve. The clock is about to strike midnight in the first time zone. Over the next twenty-four hours, as midnight sweeps around the globe, billions of people will send messages, make video calls, post photos, stream music, share videos, and wish each other well, in every language, on every platform, from every corner of the planet. The surge begins in the Pacific and rolls westward, each time zone adding its own wave of activity to a global tide of data.

At the peak, the world's cloud infrastructure is handling traffic at a scale that would have been unimaginable twenty years ago. Billions of messages. Hundreds of millions of video calls. Millions of hours of streaming. All simultaneous. All crossing the same networks, processed by the same data centers, delivered by the same CDNs.

And for you, standing in a living room somewhere, it feels like nothing. You tap your phone, send a message, see it delivered.

You join a video call and see your family's faces. You stream a song and dance. It all works. It feels simple. It feels instant. It feels like the whole system was built just for you.

In a way, it was. The cloud scales so that every user, in every moment, experiences the system as if they're the only one using it. That is the real achievement of elastic scale, not just handling billions of requests, but making each one feel personal.

Next comes the economics behind all of this: why the cloud became the dominant model for computing, why so many services are free, and what that means for you as a user and a participant in the cloud economy.

CHAPTER 9

THE ECONOMICS OF THE CLOUD (IN PLAIN LANGUAGE)

Here is a question worth sitting with for a moment: why is so much of the internet free?

You can search for anything. You can send messages to anyone. You can store thousands of photos. You can get directions to anywhere on the planet. You can watch hours of video. You can read the news, check the weather, translate languages, and manage your finances, all without paying a cent.

Someone is paying for the servers. Someone is paying for the electricity, the cooling, the engineers, the cables, the buildings. You've spent the preceding chapters learning exactly how massive and how expensive this infrastructure is. So if you're not paying for it, who is? And why?

. . .

What follows answers those questions. It's about the economics of the cloud, not the kind of economics that belongs in a business school, but the kind that shapes your daily life. Why some things are free. Why others cost money. Why the cloud became the dominant model for computing. And what all of this means for you, the person tapping the screen.

Let's start with the shift that made everything else possible, because it's the single most important economic idea in the cloud.

Before the cloud, computing was something you owned. If you were a company that needed servers, you bought servers. You installed them in a room. You hired people to maintain them. You paid for the electricity, the cooling, the space, and the insurance. The servers were yours, along with all the cost, all the risk, and all the headaches that came with them.

This is the ownership model, and it dominated computing for decades.

The cloud replaced ownership with rental. Instead of buying servers, companies rent computing power from a cloud provider, as much as they need, for as long as they need it. The provider owns the servers, the data centers, the power systems, and the staff. The company just uses the capacity and pays a bill.

. . .

The best analogy for this shift is one most people already live with: the difference between owning a car and using a ride service.

When you own a car, you pay for the vehicle, the insurance, the maintenance, the fuel, and the parking. The car is yours twenty-four hours a day, but you probably use it for two or three hours. The rest of the time, it sits in a driveway or a parking lot, costing you money while doing nothing. You're paying for full-time access to something you use part-time.

When you use a ride service, you pay only when you need a ride. Someone else owns the car, maintains it, insures it, and fuels it. You just get in, go where you're going, and get out. If you need ten rides today, you take ten rides. If you need zero rides tomorrow, you pay nothing. You've traded the overhead of ownership for the flexibility of on-demand access.

The cloud works the same way. A company that once spent millions of dollars buying servers now spends thousands of dollars renting computing power, and only when it needs it. The waste disappears. The risk drops. The flexibility is transformative.

This shift, from owning to renting, didn't just make computing cheaper. It changed who could afford to build things.

Before the cloud, launching a digital service was expensive. You needed servers before you had a single customer. You needed infrastructure before you had revenue. You needed to guess how popular your service would be and buy enough hardware to handle it, knowing that if you guessed wrong, you'd either crash under demand or waste money on idle machines.

This meant that only well-funded companies could build at scale. The barrier to entry was measured in millions of dollars of hardware, real estate, and staff.

The cloud demolished that barrier.

Today, a team of three people can launch a service that reaches millions of users worldwide. They don't buy servers. They don't lease data center space. They don't hire operations engineers. They open an account with a cloud provider, write their software, and deploy it. If nobody uses it, they've spent almost nothing. If it goes viral overnight, the cloud scales up automatically, and the bill grows only as the audience does.

This is why the app economy exists. It's why your phone is full of services built by small teams you've never heard of. It's why innovation in digital services has accelerated so dramatically over the past fifteen years. The cloud didn't just make computing cheaper for large companies. It made it *accessible* to small ones, and to individuals, students, hobbyists, and entrepreneurs who never could have afforded to build anything under the old model.

The economic revolution of the cloud isn't just about saving money. It's about lowering the threshold of who gets to build.

But this raises the question that opened the chapter: if all of this costs money to run, why is so much of it free to you?

The answer is that "free" doesn't mean "no one pays." It means *you're not the one paying with money*. You're paying with something else.

This arrangement isn't new. It's been the dominant model for media, the original information technology, for over a century.

In the nineteenth century, newspapers discovered that they could lower their cover price dramatically, or even give the paper away, if they sold advertising alongside the articles. The readers got cheap or free news. The advertisers got access to the readers. The newspaper got paid by the advertisers. The reader was the audience. The advertiser was the customer. The content was the bait.

Radio adopted the same model in the 1920s. The broadcasts were free. You didn't pay to listen. The programs were sponsored by companies, soap manufacturers, car dealers, cereal brands, who paid for access to the audience. Television followed the same pattern in the 1940s and 1950s. Free programming, funded by commercials. The viewer paid nothing. The advertiser paid everything. The network's job was to attract the largest possible audience and sell access to it.

The internet inherited this model wholesale and supercharged it. The fundamental transaction is the same one that newspapers discovered a hundred and fifty years ago: give the audience something valuable for free, and sell the audience's attention to advertisers. What changed is the precision. A newspaper ad reached everyone who read the paper. A television commercial reached everyone watching the show. An internet ad reaches *you, specifically,* targeted based on your behavior, your interests, your demographics, and your location. That precision makes each ad far more valuable, which makes the "free" model far more profitable, which is why so much of the internet can afford to be free.

Understanding this history matters because it shows that the cloud's business model isn't a tech-industry scheme. It's the latest evolution of a commercial arrangement that has funded media for generations. The mechanism is older than computers. The scale is new.

There are three dominant versions of this model in the digital economy, and understanding them will change how you look at every app on your phone.

. . .

The first is **advertising**. This is the model behind most of the services you use for free: search engines, social media platforms, video sites, news apps. The service is free to you because advertisers are paying to reach you. The platform's job is to keep you engaged, to keep you scrolling, watching, clicking, so that it can show you ads. The more time you spend on the platform, the more ads you see, and the more money the platform makes.

In this model, your attention is the product being sold. The platform is in the business of capturing your attention and selling access to it. This shapes design decisions in ways you may not have noticed: infinite scroll, autoplay videos, notification timing, and recommendation algorithms are all, in part, strategies for keeping you on the platform longer. They work because they're built on the same cloud-powered systems you've been exploring, enormous computing resources dedicated to understanding what keeps you engaged.

This isn't a conspiracy. It's a business model. And it has produced useful services: the search engine you rely on, the video platform you enjoy, the messaging app that connects you with friends. But the tradeoff is real: when you use a free, ad-supported service, you are exchanging your attention, and, often, your behavioral data, for access.

The second model is **subscriptions**. This is the model behind streaming services, cloud storage plans, productivity tools, and a growing number of apps. You pay a monthly or annual fee, and in return, you get access to the service without ads, or with fewer of them.

In this model, your satisfaction is the product. The company makes money by keeping you happy enough to keep paying. This aligns the company's incentives with yours in a way that the advertising model doesn't. An ad-supported platform benefits when you spend more time on it, regardless of whether that time is well-spent. A subscription service benefits when you feel the service is worth what you're paying, which means it's incentivized to be useful, not just sticky.

Subscriptions have been growing across the digital economy for exactly this reason. Both users and companies have recognized that paying directly for a service creates a healthier relationship than paying indirectly through attention and data.

The third model is **freemium**, a combination of free and premium. The basic version of the service is free. More advanced features, more storage, or an ad-free experience cost money. The free users serve two purposes: they're both the audience (the service works better with more people on it) and the marketing engine (some percentage of free users will eventually upgrade to paid plans).

Freemium is the model behind many of the tools you use daily: cloud storage that gives you a few gigabytes for free and charges for more, messaging apps with optional premium features, productivity tools that are basic for free and powerful for a fee.

These three models, advertising, subscriptions, and freemium, account for the vast majority of the digital economy. Almost every app you use runs on one of them, or on some combination. Once you can identify which model an app uses, you understand its incentives, and you can make more informed decisions about how you use it.

There's one more piece of the economics puzzle that connects everything here to everything you've seen so far: economies of scale.

The cloud gets cheaper as it gets bigger. A provider that operates a hundred data centers can negotiate better electricity rates, buy hardware in larger quantities, spread engineering costs across more customers, and achieve efficiencies that a smaller provider can't match. Each additional customer makes the system marginally cheaper for everyone.

This is a well-understood economic principle, the same one that makes mass-produced goods cheaper than handcrafted ones, that makes a large grocery chain's prices lower than a corner shop's, that makes a national airline's per-seat cost lower than a regional carrier's. The fixed costs are enormous, but they're spread across so many users that the per-unit cost is tiny.

. . .

In cloud computing, this principle operates with unusual force. The fixed costs, data centers, cables, cooling systems, power infrastructure, are staggering. But once they're built, the marginal cost of serving one more user is almost nothing. The electricity to process one more search query, store one more photo, or deliver one more video is so small it barely registers. This is why cloud services can offer so much for so little, and why the "free" model works at all. The infrastructure is so vast, and the costs are spread across so many users, that advertising revenue alone can cover the expense of serving hundreds of millions of people.

But economies of scale have a consequence: they naturally favor concentration. The bigger a cloud provider gets, the cheaper and better its service becomes, which attracts more customers, which makes it even bigger, which makes it even cheaper. This is a virtuous cycle for users, better service, lower cost, but it produces a market structure where a small number of very large providers dominate. The same economic forces that make the cloud affordable also make it concentrated.

This isn't unique to the cloud. It's the same pattern that produced a handful of dominant airlines, a few major telecommunications companies, and a small number of global banks. Infrastructure businesses tend toward concentration because the economics of scale are so powerful. The pattern matters not as a moral judgment, but as a structural reality that shapes the digital world you live in. For readers whose interest extends into what that concentration means for power, governance, and society, the fifth book in this series explores it in depth. Here, it's enough to see the mechanism.

There's one final angle on cloud economics that matters for you personally, because it affects how you experience the digital world every day: cloud pricing shapes what gets built.

When computing power is cheap and abundant, certain kinds of products become possible, or inevitable. Services that rely on processing enormous amounts of data in real time (search, social media, navigation) only make economic sense when the computing cost per query is nearly zero. Services that offer unlimited storage (email, photo backup) only work when the cost of storing one more gigabyte is trivial. Services that personalize every interaction (recommendations, targeted content, adaptive interfaces) only exist because the cloud makes it economically viable to run complex algorithms for every individual user.

The cloud's economics don't just determine *how* services are delivered. They determine *what* services exist. The digital world you inhabit, the apps on your phone, the services you depend on, the experiences you take for granted, was shaped by the economics of cloud computing as much as it was shaped by the technology itself.

When computing was expensive, digital services were limited, slow, and costly. When computing became cheap, the digital world exploded. The cloud's economics didn't just change the price of technology. They changed the texture of daily life.

You are a participant in the cloud economy. Not just a user, a participant.

When you use a free service, you are exchanging your attention and your data for access to computing infrastructure that costs billions of dollars to build and operate. When you pay for a subscription, you are funding the servers, the cables, the data centers, and the engineers who keep the system running. When you upload a photo, you are adding to the global demand for storage that drives the construction of new data centers. When you stream a video, you are one of hundreds of millions of simultaneous users whose collective demand shapes the investment decisions of the world's largest technology companies.

None of this should make you feel guilty. It should make you feel informed.

Understanding the economics of the cloud doesn't mean you need to change your behavior. It means you can look at the digital world with clear eyes. When a service is free, you know why. When a service starts charging, you understand the tradeoff. When a headline announces a company's massive investment in new data centers, you can see the economic logic behind it. When someone argues about the power of large technology companies, you understand the structural forces that produced that power.

The cloud is not just a technical system. It's an economic system, one you participate in every time you pick up your phone. Understanding how it works is part of understanding the world you live in.

The final chapter returns to the people who make all of this possible. The technicians who swap drives at midnight. The cable crews who lay fiber under the ocean. The engineers who monitor dashboards and respond to alarms. The cloud is built by people, maintained by people, and kept running by people. Their story is the heart of the machine.

CHAPTER 10

THE PEOPLE WHO KEEP IT RUNNING

It's four o'clock in the morning, and a phone is buzzing on a nightstand.

The man who reaches for it has been asleep for less than three hours. He's a data center technician, one of thousands who work at facilities like the ones you've been touring. The alert on his phone is from the monitoring system: a cluster of servers in the east wing of the facility has reported a pattern of disk failures that's approaching a threshold. The automated systems have already rerouted traffic and flagged the failing drives for replacement. Nothing is down. No user has been affected. But the system wants a human to look at it, because the pattern is unusual, more failures in a shorter window than the models predicted.

He gets dressed, drives twenty minutes through empty roads, badges through the security gate, walks through the mantrap, and enters the server hall. The roar of the fans greets him like it always does. The cold hits him like it always does. He walks to the east wing, finds the affected rack, and begins pulling failed drives, each one a flat metal slab, warm to the touch, that slides out of its slot with a soft click. He replaces them with fresh drives from a supply cart, one by one, checking the indicator lights as each new drive initializes and begins rebuilding its data from the redundant copies on neighboring machines.

While he works, he notices something. The rack next to the affected one is running warmer than it should. Not dangerously warm, but warmer than the baseline. He checks the airflow. A perforated floor tile has shifted slightly, disrupting the cold-air delivery to this section. He repositions the tile, feels the cool air resume its proper flow, and makes a note in the maintenance log.

By six o'clock, the drives are replaced, the airflow is corrected, and the monitoring system shows everything green. He drives home, sleeps for a few more hours, and starts his regular shift at noon.

The millions of people whose data flows through that facility will never know any of this happened. That's the point.

You've now seen cables, data centers, power systems, cooling infrastructure, reliability engineering, storage architecture, elastic scale, and cloud economics. You've seen the physical machine that powers the digital world, the steel and silicon, the glass and copper, the light and electricity. But there's one component of this system that no diagram can capture and no metaphor fully conveys: the people.

The cloud is built by people. It is maintained by people. It is kept running, day and night, by people who care about keeping it running. Their work is largely invisible, by design, because the best-run infrastructure is the kind nobody notices. But without them, the machine stops.

Let's start on the floor of a data center, because that's where the most tangible work happens.

Data center technicians are the hands of the cloud. Their job is physical in a way that surprises people who imagine the internet as a purely digital space. They lift servers, each one weighing thirty or forty pounds, and slide them into racks. They swap hard drives, dozens of them in a shift, pulling the failed ones and clicking replacements into place with practiced precision. They run cables, copper and fiber, threading them through trays and conduits, connecting new machines to the network. They inspect power connections, test backup systems, and walk the floor during rounds, checking for anything that the automated monitoring might miss.

The work requires a particular temperament. Data centers are loud, cold, and repetitive. The server halls are not designed for human comfort; they're designed for machine performance. A technician might spend hours in an environment that's sixty-five degrees, surrounded by the constant drone of fans, under fluorescent lighting that makes everything look the same shade of institutional gray. The work is methodical: check this rack, replace this drive, trace this cable, log this change. It demands attention to detail without much variety, and patience without much recognition.

But the best technicians develop something that no automated system can replicate: intuition. They hear a fan that's spinning slightly off-pitch and know a bearing is failing before the sensor catches it. They notice a cable that's been routed too close to a heat exhaust and move it before it becomes a problem. They see a pattern in the failure logs, three drives from the same manufacturing batch failing in the same week, and flag it before it becomes a cluster. This kind of human perception, built on years of experience walking the same floors and touching the same machines, is one of the reasons data centers run as well as they do.

If the technicians are the hands of the cloud, the network engineers are its nervous system.

Network engineers don't work on the physical floor as often. Their domain is the flow of data: the traffic patterns, the routing decisions, the performance metrics that determine whether your request reaches a server in forty milliseconds or four hundred. They monitor dashboards that show real-time maps of data flowing across networks, watching for congestion, latency spikes, packet loss, or routing anomalies.

Their work is analytical and reactive. On a quiet day, a network engineer might spend hours optimizing a routing configuration to shave a few milliseconds off response times for users in a particular region, the kind of improvement no individual user would ever notice, but that matters at the scale of hundreds of millions of requests. On a bad day, they might spend hours diagnosing a cascading failure, tracing the chain of events backward from user-visible symptoms to root cause, coordinating with teams across multiple facilities to isolate the problem and restore service.

The worst moments in a network engineer's life are the outages, the incidents that make headlines, that affect millions of users, that turn a routine shift into an adrenaline-fueled race to restore service while the whole world watches. These events are rare, as the reliability engineering made clear, but when they happen, the engineers at the center of them carry enormous responsibility. The decisions they make in the first few minutes, which systems to isolate, which changes to roll back, which traffic to reroute, determine whether an incident lasts thirty minutes or six hours.

After the incident is resolved, these same engineers lead the post-mortem process, the unflinching analysis of what went wrong, what was missed, and what needs to change. The best engineers approach post-mortems not as assignments of blame but as opportunities for the system to learn. Every outage, analyzed honestly, makes the next one less likely. This culture of learning from failure, of treating every incident as a teaching moment rather than a scandal, is one of the cloud industry's most valuable and least visible practices.

Now let's leave the data center entirely and go somewhere most people have never imagined: the deck of a cable-laying ship, somewhere in the middle of an ocean.

The crews who lay and repair undersea cables do some of the most physically demanding and geographically isolated work in the entire cloud infrastructure chain. A cable-laying voyage can last weeks or months. The ship moves slowly, a few miles per hour, along a predetermined route, paying out cable from enormous tanks below deck. The crew works in shifts, monitoring the cable as it feeds over the stern and sinks toward the seabed thousands of feet below.

When a cable breaks, and this happens regularly, a repair ship is dispatched to the site. The crew drags a grapnel along the ocean floor to hook the cable and haul it to the surface, a process that can take days depending on the depth and the conditions. Once the cable is on deck, the damaged section is cut out and a new section is spliced in, glass fibers aligned with microscopic precision, on a ship that's rolling in open ocean, in conditions that would make most people seasick within the hour.

. . .

These crews are specialists. The splice technicians who align the fibers are among the most skilled craftspeople in the telecommunications industry. Their work happens in a small, climate-controlled van on the ship's deck, a bubble of precision in the middle of an environment that is anything but precise. A single misaligned fiber can degrade the performance of the entire cable. The stakes are high, the conditions are difficult, and the work is invisible to the billions of people whose data will eventually flow through the repaired line.

There's a strange poetry in this: the most advanced communication system in human history depends, at its most critical moments, on a handful of people with steady hands, on a ship in the middle of the ocean, doing work that hasn't changed in its essential character since the telegraph era.

Back on land, there's another category of workers who are easy to overlook: the people who build and expand the physical infrastructure of the internet in your own neighborhood.

The fiber crews who dig trenches along suburban streets, threading glass cable through conduits that will carry your data for the next thirty years. The tower climbers who scale cell towers, sometimes hundreds of feet high, in wind and weather, to install, maintain, and upgrade the antennas that connect your phone to the network. The utility workers who splice fiber in underground vaults, working in confined spaces lit by headlamps, connecting new buildings and neighborhoods to the grid.

. . .

This work is construction: hard, physical, outdoor labor that runs on schedules dictated by weather, permits, and municipal regulations. It's the kind of work that leaves calluses and sore backs, that happens in plain sight on your street and yet remains functionally invisible to the people who benefit from it. You see the orange cones and the work trucks, maybe a trench cut into the pavement with a crew gathered around it, and you drive past without a second thought. But what's happening in that trench is the extension of the cloud into your life, a new fiber connection that will carry your voice, your photos, and your memories for decades to come.

Behind all of these visible roles, the technicians, the engineers, the cable crews, the construction workers, there is a vast support ecosystem that most people never see at all.

The manufacturing workers who assemble servers in factories, soldering components to circuit boards, testing each unit before it ships. The logistics teams who coordinate the movement of hardware from factories to data centers, sometimes across oceans, sometimes across continents, ensuring that the right equipment arrives at the right facility at the right time. The facilities managers who oversee the physical plant of a data center, the generators, the cooling systems, the electrical infrastructure, ensuring that the building itself remains a safe, reliable environment for the machines inside it.

. . .

The security teams who monitor the physical perimeter and the digital boundaries of every facility. The procurement specialists who negotiate contracts for electricity, land, and hardware at scales that would be staggering to most businesses. The compliance teams who ensure that data centers meet local, national, and international regulations for data handling, environmental impact, and labor practices.

The cloud is not a single industry. It's an ecosystem, a web of specialized roles and skills that spans manufacturing, construction, logistics, engineering, operations, security, and management. The machine you've been exploring is maintained by a global workforce that includes some of the most sophisticated engineers in the world and some of the most physically demanding labor in the industrial economy. Both are essential. Neither gets much recognition.

There's one more group of people worth mentioning, because they represent something important about the cloud that's easy to miss in a book focused on infrastructure: the people who design the invisible systems.

The software engineers who write the code that automates server deployment, monitors system health, and orchestrates failover when something goes wrong. The architects who design the systems that break your photo into chunks, distribute them across data centers, and reassemble them in milliseconds when you want to see it again. The security engineers who design the encryption, authentication, and monitoring systems that keep your data safe. The capacity planners who forecast demand months and years in advance, ensuring that new data centers are built and new cables are laid before the world needs them.

These people never touch a server. They may never set foot in a data center. But the systems they design are what make the cloud work at scale, what allow tens of thousands of machines to operate as a single, coherent system, serving billions of users simultaneously, with a reliability that borders on the miraculous.

Their work is pure abstraction, logic and code and system design, but it runs on the physical infrastructure you've been exploring from the start. The software rides on the hardware. The code rides on the cables. The architecture rides on the electricity and the cooling and the concrete. This is the complete picture of the cloud: physical machines, powered by electricity, connected by cables, maintained by technicians, coordinated by software, designed by engineers, and used by you.

Every layer depends on every other layer. Remove any one, and the system doesn't work.

What all of these people have in common is simple: they keep things running.

. . .

That sounds unremarkable, but it's one of the most undervalued forms of work in any society, and one of the oldest.

Every great infrastructure system in history has depended on a class of workers whose job was not to build the system, but to keep it going after it was built. The Roman Empire's roads were maintained by dedicated crews who filled ruts, cleared landslides, and replaced worn paving stones, year after year, generation after generation, long after the engineers who designed the roads were gone. The telegraph system of the nineteenth century depended on linesmen who climbed wooden poles in every kind of weather to repair breaks, replace insulators, and keep the wires taut, the same wires that carried the news and commerce of a nation. The telephone network of the twentieth century was maintained by operators, lineworkers, and technicians who kept millions of connections alive through storms, equipment failures, and the relentless growth of demand.

These workers rarely made history. You won't find their names in textbooks. They didn't invent the systems they maintained. But without them, those systems would have decayed within years. The Roman roads would have crumbled. The telegraph would have gone silent. The telephone network would have collapsed under its own complexity. Infrastructure doesn't maintain itself. It never has. The people who maintain it are as essential as the people who built it, and far less visible.

The data center technician who replaces drives at four in the morning belongs to this lineage. So does the cable repair crew splicing fiber in the Pacific. So does the network engineer who spends a weekend optimizing a routing table, or the security guard who checks badges at an unmarked building in the desert, or the electrician who tests backup generators once a month, every month, whether they're needed or not.

The cloud runs on maintenance. It always has. And the tradition of invisible labor that keeps it running stretches back not decades but centuries, to every civilization that built something worth preserving and then entrusted its preservation to people whose work would go unnoticed if it was done well.

This work is invisible by design. The better it's done, the less anyone notices. The highest compliment you can pay a cloud operations team is that you never think about them, because that means everything is working.

But now you know they're there. Now you know what the cloud looks like from the inside, not just the machines and the cables, but the people who walk the floors, climb the towers, splice the fibers, write the code, and respond to the alarms.

The cloud is not an abstraction that floats above human life. It is a product of human labor, built, maintained, and kept alive by people who show up, every day and every night, to make sure the machine keeps running.

. . .

The next time you tap your phone and get an answer in half a second, you're not just using a network of cables and servers. You're benefiting from the work of millions of people, most of whom you'll never meet, in places you'll never visit, doing work you'll never see.

Now you know they exist. And that completes the picture.

YOU CAN SEE IT NOW

CONCLUSION

You started this book with a cloud.

Not a real cloud, a metaphor. A word people use to describe something they can't quite picture, a vague gesture toward "somewhere out there" where their photos go and their email lives and the internet somehow happens. The cloud was abstract, invisible, and faintly mysterious, a thing you used every day without understanding, like a machine hidden behind a curtain.

The curtain is open now.

You've seen what's behind it. Not all of it, no single book could show you all of it, but enough to change the way you see the digital world for the rest of your life.

You know what the cloud is: computing that happens somewhere else, on powerful machines in buildings you've never visited, connected to your device by the internet. You know that this simple idea, work that used to happen on your device now happens on someone else's machine, became the foundation of modern digital life because it replaced the waste of ownership with the efficiency of shared infrastructure. You can explain the cloud to anyone, in one sentence, without jargon or hesitation.

You've followed the journey of a single tap, from your fingertip through the air to a local antenna, across a chain of routers, through the internet's address book, into a data center where a load balancer directed your request to the right machine, where a server verified your identity and found what you asked for, and sent the response back along a different path, through different cables and routers, to the screen in your hand. The whole trip took less than a second. You'll never look at your phone quite the same way again.

You've seen the roads that carry your data. Fiber-optic cables thinner than a garden hose, lying on the floor of the ocean, carrying nearly all the world's international internet traffic as pulses of light through glass threads. Cable-laying ships crawling across the sea for months. Repair crews splicing fibers with microscopic precision on rolling decks. The backbone, the middle mile, the last mile: the tree of infrastructure rooted in the ocean and branching into every corner of the inhabited world.

You've been inside a data center. You've felt the cold, heard the roar, seen the blinking lights stretching into the distance. You know what a server rack looks like, why the rows face alternating directions, and why everything, everything, is built with a backup. You understand that these buildings are factories, as real and as essential as any power plant or water treatment facility.

You've confronted the energy question honestly. You know that data centers consume electricity comparable to small cities, that every watt becomes a watt of heat, and that cooling is one of the great engineering challenges of the digital age. You know about the diesel generators and the battery banks that keep the machines running when the grid fails. And you know that the industry is investing, earnestly if imperfectly, in renewable energy, efficiency, and sustainability.

You've learned why the internet almost never goes down, and why it occasionally does. Redundancy, failover, monitoring, geographic distribution, and a culture that treats every failure as a lesson. The system works not because nothing breaks, but because it's designed to keep working when things do break.

You know where your stuff lives. Your photos, broken into chunks, stored in three places at once, encrypted, indexed, available on any device you pick up. Safer than any single device you own. Safer than any photograph has ever been in the history of photography.

You've grasped the concept of elastic scale, the cloud's ability to grow and shrink with demand, serving billions of people simultaneously while making each one feel like the only user. And you've understood the economics that drive it all: the shift from owning to renting, the three business models behind "free," the economies of scale that favor concentration, and the way cloud pricing shapes what gets built.

And you've met the people. The technicians who swap drives at four in the morning. The cable crews who splice fiber in the middle of the Pacific. The tower climbers and trench diggers and network engineers and software architects. The millions of people whose invisible labor keeps the machine running so that your experience of it feels effortless.

That's the cloud. Not a metaphor. Not a mystery. A machine — vast, physical, human, and real.

It is made of glass and copper, steel and concrete, electricity and light. It stretches across oceans and under streets. It hums in windowless buildings in places most people will never see. It is maintained by people who care about keeping it running, and it serves billions of users who never think about it at all.

You are one of those users. But you're a different kind now. You're the kind who can picture what happens when you tap your phone. You're the kind who understands why the internet is fast in some places and slow in others, why some services are free, why outages make the news, and why the cloud keeps getting bigger. You're the kind who reads a headline about data centers or undersea cables or energy consumption and understands what it means, because you've seen the system from the inside.

That understanding is worth more than you might think. Not because it changes what you do with your phone; you'll still tap, scroll, stream, and search the same way you always have. But because it changes what you *see*. The digital world is no longer a black box. It's a system you can reason about, evaluate, and think clearly about. And in a world that's increasingly shaped by digital infrastructure, that clarity is a form of power.

This book is the first in a series, and the foundation it built is the foundation everything else rests on.

The second book takes the infrastructure you now understand and connects it to the things you do every day: messaging, streaming, social media, maps, smart homes, notifications. You'll discover the hidden choreography behind every app you use, and you'll understand why your digital life works the way it does.

The third book addresses the question that naturally follows: how do you protect yourself? Security, privacy, passwords, scams, and the simple habits that keep you safe, explained calmly, clearly, and without fear.

The fourth book tackles the subject on everyone's mind: artificial intelligence. What it is, how it learns, why it depends on the cloud, how it's changing work, and what it can't do. No hype. No panic. Just clarity.

And the fifth book zooms all the way out and asks what the cloud means for the world: power, culture, inequality, trust, governance, and the future of civilization itself.

Each of those books builds on this one. The cables, the data centers, the power systems, the people: they don't disappear when we move on to apps or security or AI. They're still there, underneath everything, doing the work. You'll see them now, in every chapter that follows, because you know what they look like.

One last thing.

Do you remember the building in the Oregon desert, the one from the very first page of this book? The windowless warehouse humming in the darkness at two o'clock in the morning?

It's still there. Right now, as you read this sentence, it's running. The fans are spinning. The cold air is flowing. The indicator lights are blinking green. A technician is walking the floor, or driving home after a shift, or sleeping with a phone on the nightstand in case the monitoring system calls.

And somewhere in that building, on a disk in a rack in a row, a piece of your life is humming along, a photo, a message, a document, a memory, stored, replicated, encrypted, and waiting for the moment you reach for your phone and ask for it.

You know where it is now. You know what the building looks like. You know how the cables got there, how the power stays on, how the heat gets managed, how the system keeps running, and who keeps it alive.

The cloud is not magic. It never was. It's a machine — the most extraordinary machine most people have never seen.

But you've seen it now.

And that changes everything.

ABOUT THE AUTHOR

Eustace Asanghanwa is a technologist with decades of experience spanning industries from cybersecurity to cloud infrastructure to artificial intelligence. A bridge-builder between complex systems and the people they affect, he writes to empower readers with the understanding they need to navigate, and shape, the systems that define modern life. He is also the creator of the *Future Mobility Made Clear*, *Air Travel Made Clear*, and *Money Made Clear* series.

linkedin.com/in/eustacea

Made in the USA
Monee, IL
04 November 2026

67381196R00095